HOW TO GET WHAT YOU WANT FROM ALMOST ANYBODY

HOW TO GET WHAT YOU WANT FROM ALMOST ANYBODY

T. SCOTT GROSS

Health Communications, Inc.
Deerfield Beach, Florida

Library of Congress Cataloging-in-Publication Data

Gross, T. Scott.
    How to get what you want from almost anybody : your self-defense consumer guide / T. Scott Gross.
       p.   cm.
    ISBN 1-55874-371-5
    1. Customer services. 2. Consumer education. I. Title.
HF5415.5.G758 1995
658.8'12—dc20   95-46920
                                                         CIP

Publisher: Health Communications, Inc.
               3201 S.W. 15th Street
               Deerfield Beach, Florida 33442-8190

Cover redesign by Ileana Wainwright

Contents

Acknowledgments

Merry Clark made the book better with her careful, joyful editing.

My brothers, Stuart and Paul, gave me the time to write this book by shepherding our restaurant without much support from me.

Our office support, including Betty (Mom), Donna, Kay and Julie, kept the world at bay and handled all the details.

My son, Rodney, gave me lots of tips on negotiating. He should be listed as coauthor.

And thousands of smiling faces everywhere have honored me with excellent service and great ideas. But it is Melanie, my best friend, partner, and wife, who gets the most credit because she is my reason for being.

Introduction

Two stories, both true. One you've heard as a joke — but I saw it happen!

The airport was crowded, as usual, and the gentleman in line ahead of me was being anything but gentle. "Rude, arrogant, and pushy" would be the most polite description of his behavior as he harangued the unbelievably patient agent. He wanted a guarantee that he would make his connection, demanded a better seat on a completely booked flight, and insisted that the agent call to check on his request for a special meal.

When it was my turn, I said to the still-smiling agent, "I bet you would have liked to send that turkey farther than Dallas."

"It was tempting" — he grinned — "but I did put his luggage on a lovely flight to Chicago!"

At the gate, I decided to upgrade to first class. American Airlines awards AAdvantage Gold frequent fliers with a limited supply of stickers good for a space-available free upgrade. One sticker is good for up to one thousand miles of travel.

"Good morning. Do you suppose you can find room for me in first class from Dallas to Minneapolis?"

"I think so. We also have room on the San Antonio – to – Dallas leg, if you want."

"No — I really hate to waste a sticker on such a short flight. But I really will appreciate your help with that second segment."

The agent tapped into the computer and in an instant asked, "Mr. Gross, would you prefer window or aisle?"

1

"It doesn't matter. I'm so happy to be upgraded. Why don't you give me the least-preferable seat? Save the good ones for the fussy folks."

He smiled, tapped some more, and asked, "Row three or row five?"

"Really, anywhere is just fine. I'm flexible. In fact, you probably haven't met anyone as flexible as me."

"Not this morning, and certainly not among our AAdvantage Gold passengers."

I watched with a smile as the agent apparently decided to give me a "nice guy" discount and removed only one sticker for the Dallas-Minneapolis flight, a segment that I think probably required two stickers. While he worked on my boarding passes, the agent continued our pleasant conversation and in a most diplomatic way indicated that usually the most pampered upper echelon of frequent fliers were also among the most difficult.

This agent wasn't the first to make that comment. I'd heard it before, from a Delta agent in Seattle. I don't know why, but it surprised me that the folks who fly most often wouldn't have lofty manners to accompany their lofty status.

I thanked the agent and accepted my boarding passes with a smile, then stood near the door, waiting for the boarding announcement.

When I stepped on board, I was surprised to hear the flight attendant say, "Good morning, Mr. Gross. You'll be in Five E."

"Five E," I thought. "He must have given me the bulkhead seat at the front of the coach section."

Wrong. Five E was first class. For a single upgrade sticker, I was checked into first class for the entire flight. I'm known for naming unexpected, outstanding service "Positively Outrageous Service." It's service that's a surprise, a pleasant surprise, for the customer — and definitely I had just received a good dose of it. Still, I couldn't help but think about why I was sitting comfortably enjoying first-class seating . . . as well as the thought of someone else's bags being loaded on the plane to Chicago.

My job in life is to tell business people how to get ordinary folks to give Positively Outrageous Service. But everywhere I go, people who have read the book can't wait to ask, "How do I get some of this Positively Outrageous Service for me?"

The short answer's simple. For the nuances, you'll have to read on, but for now, two key points. First, if you want really great service, you must recognize that you are in a power relationship and it's the server who has the most power. Second, you must learn how to market yourself to the server.

Some might reasonably argue that this sounds unfair and that the customer shouldn't have to work to get service that should be included in the price. They are right. But what do you want most? Is it the thrill of knowing that you are absolutely right, or would you be willing to sacrifice a bit of righteousness in exchange for pleasant, hassle-free service? If you are in the "life's too short" group, stand by to learn the tricks of a professional customer as practiced by the original "Mr. Nice Guy" himself!

ONE

How to Get What You Want

1 The Persuasive Art

WHEN we moved to the country, neighbors and townfolk affectionately referred to us as "the newlyweds" who moved out along Verde Creek. That's no surprise. After seventeen years of marriage, we are still frequently mistaken for newlyweds.

To our neighbors, the sight of Melanie and me walking hand in hand nearly every evening along our country road pretty much begs such a conclusion. People still remark about how well we get along, despite our working together in cramped quarters, and that we never seem to fight.

Of course we fight! But we have a secret technique that makes fighting short, sweet, almost fun.

The same secret of interpersonal communication is responsible for the fact that nearly everywhere we go, we get great customer service. We are frequently amazed to hear horror stories about this airline or that restaurant, this teacher or that clerk.

At first we thought maybe we were just lucky. Now we know — we really do get great service, just as we really do get along like newlyweds. *How to Get What You Want from Almost Anybody* focuses on customer service.

The secret is simple. Four straightforward steps to good communication work in business and commerce as well as they've worked for us in love and marriage.

Four Steps — One Secret

The secret of getting what you want from almost anybody lies in these four steps:

- Recognize the power relationship.
- Market yourself.
- Ask for exactly what you want.
- Reward good results.

Recognize the power relationship

Service providers of all types are in a power relationship with the customer. Understanding that power relationship, and the power relationships within the organization with which you are dealing, makes all the difference in getting what you want.

At the first level, the clerks or other employees (whether you can see them or not) sit in a box, surrounded on all sides by corporate policies and procedures. Their ability to move is often highly restricted. They have severely limited power, or options, when responding to your needs.

Inside the box, the clerk remains quite secure, and may enjoy hiding behind policy and procedure to deny you the service you want, perhaps desperately need. But frequently they can be persuaded to risk stepping out of that box to help you.

RECOGNIZE THE POWER OF A CLERK TO MAKE YOUR TRANSACTION WONDERFUL OR ABSOLUTELY MISERABLE.

Even with awesome power, first-level employees frequently cannot give you the service that you want. We're not talking "will not" here. We're talking "cannot."

The smart consumer recognizes multiple power relations, enlists the assistance of persons at all levels of power, and deals directly with the level where the power lies and can deliver.

Get that? Cultivate allies at all power levels, but deal where you can get results. In other words:

DEAL WITH DECISION MAKERS.

This is especially important when you request service that is outside the norm — as simple as approval to pay by check or as unusual as special financing. Whatever the case, dealing with an employee who cannot, by policy, honor your request is a waste of time and frustrating for everyone.

Old saying: Never teach a pig to sing. It wastes your time and irritates the pig.

Market yourself

Sales are everything, and everything is sales. We forget that businesses attempting to sell us products and services are only half of the equation. When we want service that surpasses the mediocre norm, even though the customer may always be right, there is no guarantee that requests for special service will automatically be granted. Great service often requires a bit of salesmanship on the part of the customer.

Sometimes you must sell people on the idea of giving you what you want.

In a busy world, people have thousands of options about how they will spend their time and energy. Just as billboards, TV and radio commercials, and printed ads compete for attention, so must consumers who want anything other than the strictly ordinary. And who wants ordinary service, which is too often inadequate, cold, and impersonal?

As I write, a male cardinal perches proudly on top of our bird feeder. His feathers are bright red, and he sings a catchy tune. What does he have in mind? Well, a mate, of course. But since there are plenty of cardinals on the property, he knows that if he intends to get what he wants, he must do something to stand out.

Sometimes getting good service is nothing more than flirting.

Flirting may be nothing more than a friendly invitation to play. You can flirt with your spouse, a stranger, even an audience. But unless you really mean it, flirting can be just another way to make a fool of yourself.

You could say that to get what you want from almost anybody, you should be a great lover. Great lovers love unconditionally. They love friends and strangers alike. They even love the unlovable.

Okay, maybe I've gone just a bit overboard. Then again, maybe not. It works for me!

RECEPTIONIST: *Good morning! Region Three office.*

CALLER: *And good morning to you! How come you're so cheerful today?*

RECEPTIONIST: *It must be spring.*

CALLER: *Well, connect me to Steve, and then take the rest of the day off.*

RECEPTIONIST: *I wish!*

CALLER: *Don't worry, I'll write you an excuse.*

RECEPTIONIST: *I don't think they'll fall for that one, Scott.*

CALLER: *How'd you know it was me?*

RECEPTIONIST: *Your mustache!*

Ask for exactly what you want

Ask and ye shall receive

When you carefully examine instances in which people are dissatisfied with goods or services, you realize that they didn't ask for what they expected to receive.

ASK FOR EXACTLY WHAT YOU WANT.

Sometimes, if what you want is out of the ordinary, it's helpful to go the extra step and tell why you are asking: "Would you mind leaving a pitcher of water on the table? I'm very thirsty, and it will save me from having to ask and you from making a dozen trips."

Reward good results

Ever wonder why one child goes to bed when told and another throws a tantrum? Simple: You get what you reward. One parent rewards going to bed; the other rewards tantrum throwing.

"Let's see if I've got this straight," muses the two-year-old. "I fall to the floor and kick and scream, and she will pick me up, feed me ice cream, and let me stay up. Yep! That's the ticket!"

People aren't stupid. They just do stupid things because somehow those stupid things get rewarded.

Want stupid behavior? Reward stupid behavior.

Want great service? Reward great service.

Later we'll learn how customers reward bad service or sometimes miss opportunities to encourage great service. For now, just remember that not only do you get what you reward — you get what you deserve!

I commented to one of our delivery drivers that he seemed to be doing an extra-thorough job of checking to see that the order he was about to deliver was complete.

He smiled. "Ferris Rental."

"What about them?"

Bigger smile, followed by "Bi-i-i-g tippers!"

REWARD GOOD RESULTS.

"Thank you! That was great service!" works pretty well. So does a handsome tip. So does a card, letter, or phone call to the boss, or a surprise bouquet of flowers. The results you reward determine the results you get.

Recognize the power relationship:

ME: *Hi! Just the guy we need to make this a great evening.*

SERVER: *Well, I'm Chris, and looks like you guessed I'm your waiter.*

Market yourself:

ME: *Nice to see you, Chris. I'm Scott, and this is my backup group. We are your customers!*

Ask for exactly what you want:

WAITER: *Great! Are you ready to order?*

ME: *Yes. We have to catch an eight o'clock flight, so tonight we need you to hold back on the usual elegant service and get us out as quickly as possible.*

SERVER: *No problem. I'll take both your drink and food order now if you're ready. Then I'll get salads right away. Just let me know if you feel rushed.*

ME: *Perfect!*

Reward results:

ME: *(Generous tip added to check with this note handwritten across the face: "We really appreciated your fast service. Next time we'll be sure to ask for you. Thanks!")*

Getting what you want from almost anybody is not difficult. I have many more tips that you can use to move from amateur to pro, but in the end it all comes down to:

- Recognize the power relationship.
- Market yourself.
- Ask for exactly what you want.
- Reward good results.

TWO

Scott's Secret Strategies

2 | Assume Good Service

THE NUMBER one tip for getting good service: Assume that you are going to get what you want. When you expect Positively Outrageous Service, and communicate that expectation by your body language, tone of voice, and word choice, you establish from the outset that you are someone who is accustomed to getting good service. So long as you keep the approach friendly and unthreatening, you create an irresistible desire to give you exactly what you want.

Military people refer to this psychological-physiological positioning as Command Presence. It is not threatening, pushy, arrogant, or demanding. Rather, it is positive, powerful, expecting.

You must approach servers with a presence that communicates that you came to get great service. You won't be surprised to get great service. You won't settle for less.

Establish Command Presence in four ways: appearance, body language, tone of voice, and word choice.

Appearance is critical. In some parts of the country people "get dressed" to go shopping. Everywhere, it is still wise to dress for the task. If you don't believe it, throw on your grubbies and head for an expensive retailer. If you get service at all, it's likely to be surly and indifferent.

Repeat the experience wearing the exact same clothes but with different shoes, handbag, and jewelry. Class up the accessories and you immediately position yourself in the mind of servers as a moneyed consumer who is just dressing comfortably.

Try again, only this time dress to the nines — go all out — and observe one of nature's most basic laws in action. The word "attractive" prompts its own definition. Shop looking like a million bucks and salespeople will gravitate to you. People like to work with — want to be with — attractive people.

If you want Positively Outrageous Service, you should look as though you are worthy of special attention.

Command Presence requires strong body language. Stand tall, walk briskly, and look clerks straight in the eye when you approach. March in as if you own the joint, as if you are someone important. Communicate exactly what you expect.

It is difficult to describe the difference between asking confidently and demanding arrogantly. But believe me, both you and the server will know instantly if you've stepped over the line.

Command Presence is a remarkable ability.

Many years ago my dad was transferred from his job as a restaurant manager for Frisch's Big Boy to the same position in another restaurant in the chain. Walking through the kitchen door on his first day, he was appalled to see that the kitchen was filthy. He continued into the dining room, where he introduced himself and immediately began ingratiating himself with the crew by helping with morning setup.

Everything went fine until Dad got a close look at the paper coasters that went with each fresh cup and saucer set. "Frisch's Big Boy" definitely was not the name printed on the coaster. Had he come to the right place? To double-check, he eased over to the window and looked at the huge outdoor sign.

"Toto, I don't think we're in Kansas anymore. And we definitely aren't at Frisch's."

Dad quickly excused himself and headed for the back door. On his way through the kitchen, appalled anew by the filth, he suddenly stopped and said to the morning cook, "I'll be back in less than an hour. And when I get back, I want this kitchen looking sharp."

Command Presence.

Just before what would turn out to be a rainy dawn, unable to sleep and with a few hours to kill before flying home from Los Angeles, I pointed the car toward Venice Beach to watch morning slip up on one of my favorite California towns. At one point, I noticed two people. He was tall — my guess would be well over six foot six — and he outweighed her by at least a hundred pounds. She was small, and struggling to escape his grip.

I drove past them, rationalizing the incident as a simple marital squabble. Then I reconsidered, stepped on the brake, and shifted into reverse.

As I stepped into a rain-filled gutter, a man called from a street-side apartment: "Help her, dude. He's trying to kidnap her."

"Call the police!" I shouted, then gritted my teeth and commanded, *"Get out here!"*

By now they were twenty feet farther down the sidewalk. She was screaming. He was cursing. He looked much larger close up. It was cool, but I started to sweat.

Then a funny thing happened: Command Presence. I firmly clasped my hand around a huge wrist and, equally firmly, commanded, "Let go."

Then a miracle happened. He did.

I was surprised. She was surprised. He was surprised.

I pulled her, still screaming, to my car. As I jumped in on the driver's side, a hairy arm reached through the passenger-side window in an attempt to unlock the door. (Apparently, Command Presence does not have an indefinite shelf life.) I didn't know if I should fumble to find the electric window control or drive. I did both, and we escaped unharmed.

The point of the story: If Command Presence can foil a kidnapper, just imagine what it can achieve with a difficult salesclerk!

3

Service Is a Laughing Matter

"**M**ARKETING" is a big-business word for a common concept. The idea behind marketing: Do something that makes a product (or in this case a person) stand out in the mind of the customer. Okay, so you're ahead of me. Folks who get Positively Outrageous Service mentally trade places with the server.

To get really wonderful service — service above and beyond the ordinary — the customer must do something to attract the server's attention. Celebrities, naked people, and folks with extensive tattoos don't have to worry about attracting attention. The rest of us do.

"Hi! I'm Gladys Knight, and these are the Pips." Check out the cover. I'm not Gladys Knight, and I've never met the Pips. But I have, on many occasions, introduced myself to restaurant servers just that way. Sometimes I use real names, particularly in places where servers are required to introduce themselves by name (which is usually Biff).

"Good evening. My name is Biff, and I'll be your server tonight."

"Hiya, Biff. I'm Scott, and this is Melanie, Joe, and Joyce. We'll be your customers."

A little humor right from the beginning usually relaxes the server and communicates that you're going to be a fun group to serve. Face it, servers have plenty of choices about how to spend their time. Overworked servers can stay constantly busy and never make it to your table at all. Say something funny or even just plain friendly and the server will want to be near your table.

Chances are your fun approach will even be remembered and get you great service on your next visit, without much work on your part at all.

The Candy Man

A long-distance trucker called in to a late-night radio talk show to tell me about his adventures as the "Candy Man." He had developed the habit of giving hard candy to the truckstop waitresses across the country who served him at all hours.

The Candy Man was an "equal-opportunity tipper" — he made certain that everyone on duty, from cook to table clearer to hostess, got one of his sweet treats. He was not a big tipper in terms of cash, but what kind of service do you think he got? Positively Outrageous Service, for the price of a few pieces of candy.

Any time you do something just a little bit out of the ordinary, people remember. Whether introducing yourself as Gladys Knight or adopting a persona like the Candy Man, you gain attention — the first step in getting what you want from almost anybody.

I fell into my seat on United's early-evening flight from Denver to San Antonio. Contacts had been replaced by glasses, and my near-trademark red tie had been stuffed into a pocket.

That wasn't enough to keep the passenger next to me from casting inquiring glances in my direction.

Earlier that morning I had been interviewed on Denver's KUSA morning news. The anchor had asked for a quick tip on how to get better service in a restaurant. I had responded by telling how the evening before we had used the Gladys Knight bit.

Now, climbing to cruising altitude, my seatmate just couldn't resist.

He smiled. "I know you — I saw you on the news this morning. You're Gladys Knight!"

I stopped at a pay phone to make my usual Saturday telephone call to my gran in Kentucky. It turned out to be a non-AT&T phone. But after I dialed the access code, a pleasant, professional voice said, "AT&T. May I help you?"

"Yes, ma'am! It's Saturday, time to call Granny. Here's the magic number." I recited my phone card number and then said, "I'll tell Gran you helped with the call. Thanks, and Merry Christmas!"

There was a slight pause, followed by "Thank you! I'll make certain you get the direct-dial rate . . . and Merry Christmas to you!"

Being playful doesn't cost a cent. At the very least, it brightens your day. More often than not, when you take time to play, you get more than service — you get involvement.

It was late. I was late. It didn't take more than a glance at the parking lot to see that the motel was full. Still, it wouldn't hurt to try.

"Hi! I sure hope you can find room for one more skinny guy. It looks like you're pretty close to full. I bet you're having a heck of a day, too."

She barely looked up, but there was a hint of a smile.

Bingo! I could smell victory.

"I was six foot six and handsome when I started out this morning."

She pushed aside her paperwork and, in a teensy flirt back, said, "So you're not six foot six."

"Hey, you're all right!"

"And you're in luck. So you won't have to worry about getting any shorter, I've got a room around the corner. It's a suite, but since you're such a nice guy, you can have it for the single rate."

If being a customer requires patience and presence, just imagine how tough life can be for the server . . .

There was something special about the new server at Denny's, where I was working during college. She had lost a job as an animal trainer at an outdoor wild animal park. (A flash flood had washed out half of the park.)

On her first day, she did something that proved it takes special people to handle the public.

I'll never forget it (and neither will she). A family was seated at a table near the window. It was late in the afternoon, and her trainer had gone on break, leaving the new kid to take her first solo order. I was watching from the kitchen when she greeted the guests, bending slightly to listen to their order. In a flash, her panties slid down to her ankles.

I would have just disappeared from the universe. She just excused herself, straightened to full height, and shuffled over to the service island. Carefully she stepped out with one foot, then lifted the other until she could slide her underwear off her ankle. She dropped it daintily into her pocket and went back to taking the order!

Service people work hard and take a lot of guff. You never know what ups and downs they've endured . . . give 'em a break!

4 | Everybody Loves a Chameleon

SERVICE workers take a lot of crap.

Their customers phone it in, fellow employees haul it in, and bosses seem to enjoy mailing it in. So it's not surprising to run into a server who seems to be just itching for a fight. Sometimes, because of good training or residual good manners, your server won't be openly hostile. But pay attention and you'll see those little cracks around the edges.

A server who is just not having a great day creates an opportunity to empathize. You can pretty much guess what's bothering folks, so jump right in and join their anger or frustration. When someone is really in the pits, the last thing they want is to deal with someone who seems terminally happy. Sometimes that can be a gap too difficult to bridge simply by turning up the humor.

For example, your server has just been emotionally mugged by a series of cranky customers, and then a supervisor in a lilting whisper leaves the word "Smile" echoing in her ear.

What should be your approach? The smart customer will

adopt the emotion of the moment, lean in close, and say, "Pretty rough day, isn't it?"

Don't say it with a silly grin. Instead, show a little disgust, as if you had experienced the treatment. The server will immediately recognize you as an ally and quickly vent frustration or anger — not at you, but with you. Most of the time the moment will pass in an instant. And before long you'll be chatting like old friends, and you will be getting the service you want.

Tom Holter, a talk show host on the Sun radio network, tells this wonderful story: While waiting his turn to request seating at Scoma's, a famous San Francisco restaurant, Tom was appalled to hear the guest ahead of him attempt to bully the hostess into seating him immediately, ahead of the waiting line. When it was Tom's turn at the desk, he made a nurturing remark, something like "I hope you don't have to deal with much of that! The name is Holten, and we'll be happy to wait patiently."

With that, the hostess looked up from her list, smiled, and said, "Oh yes, Mr. Holter. Your table is ready!"

A good story became a great story a few days later. After touring the nearby wine country, Tom and his party decided that a return visit to Scoma's would be a perfect cap to their California vacation. As soon as he approached the hostess through the waiting crowd, she said, "Good evening, Mr. Holter. Your table is ready!"

5 | Power to the People

ALL GREAT salespersons are trained to seek out the decision maker. Stories of countless hours and dollars spent wooing an individual who did not have the authority to buy are legendary.

Equally frustrating to salespeople: the inability to reach that decision maker, once identified. And don't kid yourself, to get great service today the consumer must sometimes be a salesperson, too.

Often the keeper of the gate is a secretary. For the most part, secretaries are bright, competent, protective, and extremely perceptive. They are quick to anticipate the needs of the boss. They can, and will, if approached properly, provide valuable information about finances, policies, and other important details that could make the difference in whether you get what you want.

Smart salespeople recognize this source of power. They are quick to cultivate a relationship. They know that a secretary who is on your side can put in a respected good word, even place your name on the boss's appointment calendar.

Why do we consumers fail to recognize these power relationships? The cashier can often choose to accept or reject your personal check. Only the ticket agent can see the computer screen — are there really no aisle seats available? The news carrier really can hit the porch, but the rose bushes are just as easy to target.

Recognize server power and use it to your advantage. Don't be afraid to be direct.

It was one of life's little stupid moments. We simply forgot to check our flight time, and showed up at the Las Vegas airport fat, dumb, and happy, expecting to wait forty or so minutes for our flight home.

At the ticket counter, we smiled and asked, "What are the odds of this flight leaving on time?"

"I'd say just about one hundred percent, Mr. Gross. As a matter of fact, it took off exactly on schedule five minutes ago!"

Uh-oh! Our tickets were nonrefundable. There we stood, a thousand miles from home, with no tickets.

"I hope I don't look as stupid as I feel. If I beg and promise to send you the title to my car, is there any way you can get us home?"

"Of course! We have a rule just for this occasion, rule eighty-five. I'll write an excuse on your ticket, and you can hop on the first flight out in the morning!"

Lucky for us we were on Southwest Airlines. Those folks seem capable of being friendly even when the customers are not. Still, attempting to bully the agent could have produced vastly different results. If you think you have all the power in these transactions, think again.

Stuck, in Las Vegas for another night, we taxied to a hotel, put on our tourist face, and decided to make the best of our luck.

At the Aladdin, an obvious tourist introduced himself to the captain as Dr. Jones, flashed a twenty-dollar bill, and informed the captain that he wanted a table near the front. When it was our turn, we said a friendly hello to our captain and said that we would prefer to sit close to the front but anywhere would be fine. We were seated near the doctor.

Before the show began, I cornered our captain and asked for an insider's scoop on tipping and the art of getting a good seat.

"We have to give good service. I try to satisfy the guest, and when you do that you may get a tip, even from the rude guy."

"Does the rude guy get the seat he wants?"

"With me, he gets another captain. If you're asking, do we give rude people the worst seats, the answer is no. If you're asking if nice people get the best seats, just look where you're sitting!"

Power. They've got it, and if you think you can take it by force, think again.

6 | Deny Anonymity

ONE OF the customer's greatest tools — I was going to say "weapons" — is a name tag. Big business puts name tags on employees so you can complain. Middle managers love to respond to complaint letters that mention the offending employee by name.

They play a game you could call "Now I've got you." Anyone looking for an excuse loves one that comes already labeled by a name tag.

That's the way too many businesses operate: *Wear the name tag . . . screw up . . . and I've got you!*

The problem is that most customers don't complain; they just go away. When service deteriorates to that point, it's a sign of failure on everybody's part. Poor service can almost always be laid at the feet of management.

Often the problem goes back to sloppy hiring practices. In fact, hiring and keeping good people is so difficult in some industries that recruiting is referred to as "body snatching." Desperate managers often use the "coroner's hiring technique": If a mirror under the applicant's nose fogs up, that's a sufficient sign of life to say "You're hired."

At our restaurant, a Church's Chicken franchise, we have two rules: First, if we can't find a winner, we don't hire — even if it means paying overtime or working short. We believe that even one loser can contaminate an entire crew, even our best winners.

Second, if we find a winner, we hire, even if the crew roster is full. Find a winner, hire them, and then figure out what to do.

Job design probably accounts for 80 percent of service problems. The person who seems rude or slovenly may be a pretty nice individual off the job. Unfortunately, employees are hired but not trained. They are required to produce but are not rewarded. The worst problems occur when management fails to clearly communicate the corporate mission — or, worse still, sends one message via positive signs and catchy slogans while at the same time sending a completely different message via their actions.

But even though these are management problems, ultimately the consumer suffers. Just understand that employees who attempt to satisfy unclear or conflicting goals or who must work in understaffed, poorly equipped operations often cannot provide good service even if their intentions are good. So keep your weapons holstered!

I'm not saying that you shouldn't do everything practical to get what you want. Rather, you can make organizational pressures to work for you.

To get good service even under difficult circumstances, use one simple trick: Deny the server anonymity. Too often, especially in large organizations, servers can get away with less than acceptable service simply by remaining anonymous.

Your tactic: In almost every service situation you should verbalize the server's name. If you have an extended interaction, go the extra mile and introduce yourself. This simple action accomplishes two goals. First, the server is put on notice that you have his or her name. Second, introducing yourself immediately elevates you above the faceless mass. In fact, the server may worry that you are either from the corporate office or someone whose name they should have remembered! Either way, introducing yourself almost guarantees good service.

True story:

"Hello, my name is Madeline. I'll be your server tonight."

"Hi, Madeline. We're Scott and Melanie, and we'll be your customers!"

"This is my first day on the job, so I'm a little nervous."

"No problem, Madeline. This is our first time here as customers, so we'll figure it out together!"

Madeline almost moved in at our table! We were the only ones who made her feel at ease.

7 | Help Yourself

SOMETIMES you're just not going to get good service. Sometimes you're lucky to be served at all. Basically, you can complain, leave, suffer, or help yourself.

Purists will argue that they pay for good service, they deserve good service, and they're not about to do anything for themselves that rightfully should be done for them. Fine. So sit there and smolder. Or walk out. Or create the biggest scene since Nicholson in *Five Easy Pieces*.

No, I definitely do not recommend the movie solution. Sweeping china onto the floor to strike out at a recalcitrant server won't get you lunch. It might get you arrested.

Walking out isn't much of an option, either. Never going back will be sufficient revenge, as will complaining to half the world. But walking out is often a much greater inconvenience to you than the simple act of helping yourself.

Complaining is a great option, but even that approach often may not be the path of least resistance.

No, sometimes you've just got to take the bull by the horns and do it yourself. Many people are reluctant to help themselves because you just aren't supposed to pour your own coffee, rummage through stock drawers, or wander into the warehouse.

What will people say if they see you doing things normally reserved for the ubiquitous "authorized personnel only"? For one thing, they just might get off their fat rumps and help you. Who cares if you get an icy glare? After all, you can feel smug knowing that you won't have to tip. You're finally getting the service you deserve, and you'll have a juicy tale to tell back at the office.

A common example of do-it-yourself service can be found in many busy restaurants during the breakfast rush. How many times have you seen an overworked, underpaid waitress racing from table to table in an attempt to take orders before customers walk out, and deliver food before it petrifies? Should you join the crowd with their hands up, trying to get her attention?

The smart customer gets up, pours coffee, and continues to enjoy breakfast. Extra-nice guys will pour a refill at nearby tables, enjoying the inevitable razzes about "getting good tips," thus turning a slow burn into an opportunity to share the moment with an admiring stranger or two.

Servers definitely do not like self-service. If they truly couldn't get to you, they will apologize while you politely smile and say, "No problem. You are obviously understaffed, and I don't mind at all." If your self-service was the result of slothful inattention, what do you care whether they like it or not?

Next time you are in a large discount store, notice the telephones that usually hang on a pole in every aisle or so. They are intended for employee use only. Usually you cannot dial out on them, but you sure can access the store PA system.

You wouldn't dare?

I would. Particularly if I just couldn't find someone to help me and I needed to get home before the end of the week.

Just pick up the phone, dial the access code (this will be posted on the phone), and say something pleasant, like "Attention, please. This is a customer, aisle B, and I can't seem to find saw blades."

You will get assistance. Immediately.

Sears was a favorite store when we were first married. On slow Saturdays, when we had nothing to do but window shop at the mall, we always hit Sears first. Some clever marketer put hardware right next to appliances. We'd hit the door and I'd turn left to browse with Mr. Craftsman. Melanie would wander around with Mr. Kenmore.

One Saturday we actually had a goal: a new couch. Walking through the appliance department en route to furniture, we were spotted by the Appliance Vultures, those pleasant-looking gentlemen who stand waiting for someone to do more than glance at a dishwasher or refrigerator.

"Washer? Dryer?" inquired the more seasoned of the pair in a lifeless monotone.

"No thanks," I replied. "I'll just hose her down when I get her home."

In the furniture department, we found the perfect sofa in minutes. But finding the sofa was considerably easier than buying it. The big money must be in appliances, because there was no one to be found in furniture.

We settled comfortably onto the couch and waited.

The phone rang. Once. Twice. Three times, and on until I lost count around twenty and took matters into my own hands.

"Good afternoon. Sears furniture department. This is a customer speaking. May I help you?"

"I'm looking for an entertainment center. What do you have?"

"This really is a customer, ma'am. But it looks like they have several nice choices. What exactly did you have in mind?"

"Something in light oak or pine. Not too tall, and maybe with enclosed cabinets at the base."

"I see two that might do the job. Give me your name and phone number. If we ever get waited on, I'll see what they can do about the price and have them call you."

"Gee, that would be great. I'm Cindy, and my number is . . . . Thanks!"

"No problem, Cindy. Thanks for calling Sears!"

Eventually an obviously overworked woman emerged from the back room, approached us, and asked if she could help.

"Yes, ma'am. We'd like to buy the couch. But first, if you can let that entertainment center go for under five hundred dollars, we need you to call Cindy and tell her you'll hold it until she can come in and see it."

"I think we can do that. Who is Cindy?"

I smiled. "One of my customers."

Here is one more story to prove the point, an article spotted in the *San Antonio Express News.*

GATLIN HELPS OUT AT BUSY EATERY

Rudy Gatlin, of country music's Gatlin Brothers, tried his hand at busing tables and taking orders when an eatery where he was having lunch got busy, the restaurant's owner says.

The singer got up and cleared tables for more than an hour Nov. 13 at Biddle's Lunch Box outside Nashville, the Nashville Banner said this week.

"He started waiting on customers, putting orders in the back. Then people started asking him for autographs," said owner Sharon Biddle, who was missing an employee because of jury duty.

"He said he'd always wanted to call an order back through a window," she said.

8 | Take Me to Your Leader

WHEN IT comes to getting your way with service people, the least successful technique is to bully or push. The world loves to hate screamers. Even when a screamer is absolutely right, other customers root against them. They have a way of making life unpleasant for everybody.

The first to yell loses. The first to smile wins.

Ordinary employees in ordinary situations have almost zero options when serving customers. Too many bosses and too many customers think clerks are idiots. Some are, but working people often possess great wisdom and insight. Unfortunately, we often fall victim to the idea that if you are working at the bottom of the hierarchy, it must be due to some sort of genetic shortcoming. Not so.

Understand that an untrained customer poking into the work of a skilled technician can be irritating, if not downright costly. Still, the best service people know that an informed customer can be a tremendous asset. The real pros take the time to keep their customers informed, and thus to keep their customers.

Bob DiFazio, owner of Mobile Car Care Center in Boston,

says, "I like to involve the customer in their service." Of course, he does not invite them to help, but he does show the diagnostic computer and treat them to a look under the hood and a preview of the work to be done.

DiFazio is a good guy. But what do you do when you aren't working with men in white hats? What do you do when the server insists on hiding behind policy to avoid solving the problem?

Never yell. Go straight to the top.

The trick to going around the server: Try to recruit the server to your cause. If that's impossible or simply unlikely, you should assume that the server is on your side and say, "Who can help *us* solve the problem?"

You may want to ease the moment: "I can see that this is a situation that may be uncomfortable to handle" or "I wouldn't want you to do anything that might get you into trouble."

The deal-killer phrase that you should avoid at all costs: "I want to talk to your boss." These words create a powerful reaction: "Oh, yeah?" Instantly you have managed to create a win-lose situation.

It's also the least effective way to actually see the boss.

"He's not in."

Sure.

When you are absolutely certain that the server either will not or cannot cooperate, simply say, "Who can we see who has the authority to say yes?" Be prepared to explain that your intentions are solely to solve a problem, not to create one. Also be prepared to repeat the phrase until at last you are certain that you have an audience with the person who has the power to say yes. Reaching the top does not guarantee a yes, but at least you are dealing with someone with the authority, if not the motivation, to solve your problem.

When the shortening-filter machine at our restaurant decided to quit, we didn't expect the repair to be complicated or to take more than a few hours. Wrong. There wasn't a spare pump motor to be found anywhere within five hundred miles.

We got the usual "We'll have to order one. It will take a few days" from the repair shop. In food service, "a few days" just won't do.

"Sorry. That's the best we can do. Besides, the factory reports none in stock. Maybe you can borrow a machine."

We went directly to the manufacturer, Dean Industries. The parts clerk at Dean was polite and professional, but her computer showed that our part was out of stock. The nicest approach in the world couldn't create a pump motor where none existed.

"I can see that this is a problem that you can't solve. Who could we talk to who might be able to help us?"

"Maybe our service manager can think of something. He's out to lunch, but I'll ask him to call you as soon as he returns."

"You won't let me down, will you?"

"I promise."

In less than thirty minutes the assistant service manager, Jay Commiskey, called and, in a conspiratorial tone, reported, "Technically, there are no pump motors to be had. But by this time tomorrow, you should receive a motor. That should solve the problem."

"Great! But since 'technically' there are no motors, just where did you locate one?"

"Our inventory shows a negative count, and somehow the guys on the assembly line are short a motor. I have no idea how that happened!"

Yelling at the parts clerk would have produced zero results. Enlisting her as an ally and then going to the top made all the difference.

9 | Take the Inside Track

FEAR IS a great consumer motivator. Fear of paying too much, fear of getting lost, fear of looking foolish in public all influence the way we behave. Reasonable or not, fear tends to run our lives. Yet most of these everyday fears can be eliminated, simply by asking.

The trick: Find someone with inside information. Job applicants have been successful simply because they asked a secretary how best to approach the boss.

Shoppers have made incredible deals simply because they found a salesperson who tipped them off to a great buy on slightly damaged merchandise. And who doesn't know a shrewd shopper who always asks, "When do you expect this to go on sale?"

Smart people take the fear out of dealing with others by asking for inside information.

If you say, "How much is the price on that television?", inevitably the answer you get is the retail price of the television. If instead you create an insider relationship, you'll be in a whole different ball game.

"I really like that TV, but I'm not sure if it's the right

decision. Are there any other deals that might make more sense to you?"

In a sense, whenever we shop in an unfamiliar store for unfamiliar products, we are as foreign as tourists in a strange town.

We know that tourists sometimes operate at a disadvantage when it's time to choose a hotel, a restaurant, or a route to view the scenery: They just don't know their way around. That's why it's always comforting to discover that you have a friend — or even a friend of a friend — who lives nearby and can give you a few inside tips.

They can tell you whether a destination lives up to its hype. They can tell you when the crowds will be smallest, maybe even how to bargain for a better seat or deal. Better yet, an insider can often provide you with an introduction that will smooth the way to better treatment or perhaps a behind-the-scenes look.

The challenge really belongs to the person who doesn't have an insider to rely on. What do you do? You create an insider relationship.

Create an insider relationship by asking for special treatment. For example, you are a movie buff, and you would really like to see how the projection and sound systems work. Ask to speak to the theater manager and request a tour.

Have the good sense not to ask at 8 P.M. on a Friday night, but do ask. You may have to use a little psychology, but it needn't be any shrewder than "I don't know if you are allowed to do this, but if it's at all possible I would love to have a quick tour of your projection booth."

At a marine park, we wanted to get a firsthand look at the whale. Within minutes of asking, we found an usher who was the best friend of a trainer, who invited us to stick around after the show for one-on-one time with a killer whale. You can't always expect this kind of service, but you will never get it until you learn to ask.

My Grandpa Gross once came to visit and offered to purchase a roast for dinner. At the market he created an insider relationship like this:

"Excuse me," he called to the butcher. "I just inherited forty thousand dollars, and I'm looking for a special roast to help us celebrate."

"What did you have in mind, sir?"

"Well, something about ten pounds, without much fat. It's not every day you inherit forty thousand dollars."

"I'd say not! Look, I have a twelve-pound roast that I was holding for the manager. I guess we could trim off two pounds of fat to get you a ten-pound, very special forty-thousand-dollar roast."

With that, he vanished into the cutting room. We watched through the glass as he prepared for delicate roast surgery. When he emerged, he held a beautiful roast, just over ten pounds and not an ounce of fat. He marked it as ten pounds, congratulated my grandfather, and told him that anytime he inherited forty thousand dollars he should come back and ask for Bill.

(Of course, Grandpa didn't inherit forty thousand dollars any more than he could fly to the moon.)

Creating an insider relationship usually is a simple matter of asking.

"This is my first visit. I'll bet you can give me a tip or two for really enjoying the park."

"I haven't been here before. What do you serve here that I wouldn't be likely to find in my home state of Texas?"

"I want to make certain to purchase the perfect _____. Can you give me some pointers?"

"Can you help me? I don't seem to be having any luck getting your boss to return my calls. What do you think would be the best approach?"

Displaying your vulnerability almost always works. "I'm new here — can you help me?" Any variation of the theme stands out as so out of the ordinary even the most hardened service people generally melt.

There is a danger in adopting this position without careful attention to your power position. If you ask for help in a wimpy, whiny manner, you are setting yourself up for mistreatment. The effective approach is to adopt a vulnerable yet in-control manner. Use that Command Presence!

10 | You're Asking for It!

WHEN IT comes to asking for service, two things are certain: Customers don't ask for what they want, and servers are not psychics.

We have an item on our menu that we call chicken tender strips: marinated boneless breast meat, lightly battered, deep-fried to a golden brown, and served with piping-hot country-style white pepper gravy for dipping. Our family-size order of twenty tenders is a favorite. But at least once a week someone confuses chicken tenders with our regular-style bone-in chicken. Without taking a good look at the menu, they ask for "the twenty-piece family order," only to call half an hour later to ask what happened to their chicken!

Getting good service requires clear communication from both parties. Perhaps our menu should be easier to understand. Perhaps our customers should pay more attention. Whatever the case, probably half of what passes for poor service is nothing more than sloppy communication.

Mr. James is a regular. The other day, he called in his order.

"Good morning, Mr. James!"

"Hi, Stu. Let me have my regular."

"Yes, sir! Will that be your regular two-piece dinner pack or your regular biscuits and gravy?"

"Biscuits. I forgot to bring my bottom teeth."

Remember, when you walk into a store you usually have a mental picture of exactly what you want. Sometimes this picture is so vivid that you forget that the clerk doesn't share it.

The other day we went to Denny's for breakfast. I ordered up a cholesterol special. "I'd like this breakfast just as it's pictured on the menu," thinking that the hash browns looked wonderfully crispy.

When she brought my order, the eggs were picture-perfect, but the hash browns were better described as hash light-browns. I wanted well-done hash browns, nice and crisp, and should have had the good sense to say so.

Occasionally I like to surprise my wife with a new dress, blouse, or other item. It may be something I saw in a magazine, or perhaps I've noticed someone wearing a particularly attractive outfit that I think would look good on Melanie.

Because I know exactly what I want, it's frustrating to have a clerk lead me with great confidence to something that couldn't possibly be it. Are they not listening? Are they trying to snooker me into buying what they have instead of what I want? Probably not. Most likely it's because I didn't tell them exactly what I wanted.

If you want excellent service, ask for it.

"I need several cedar fence boards. Would you show me where they are and help me pick them out?"

Notice how different that request is from "Can you tell me where to find cedar fence boards?"

Or try this one: "I need reservations for one night for two people. A nonsmoking room with queen-size bed is our preference. If possible, we would appreciate something on the ground floor."

Being specific beats the daylights out of "I need reservations for tomorrow night." Try that and let me know how you enjoyed the smoking room on the nineteenth floor with the view of the freeway.

Servers have choices. The less desirable product they pawn off on folks who aren't specific. They have trouble renting the room by the dumpster, selling the two-by-fours with the knots, filling the seats behind the roof columns, and serving the roast beef that's still mooing.

Not only will your failure to be specific get you less than excellent treatment, you actually run the risk of getting below-average service.

Asking for excellent service should often include a reason for the request. Giving a reason informs the server that you are not being picky just because you think you are so wonderful. There's a legitimate reason why you may need and deserve special attention.

"Would you help me load this into my car? I recently had surgery, and my doctor asked me to take it easy. I don't normally act quite so wimpy."

"Could you possibly find us an extra-quiet table? My sweetie has had a really tough day, and I think she would enjoy being away from the crowd."

"I need one of these five shirts back tomorrow. We're having a portrait taken, and this shirt is my favorite."

"Can you give me an appointment when the doctor is most likely to be on time? I understand that if he has surgery that runs long, it can put him behind schedule. Since I miss work to be here, I would appreciate it if you would schedule me for the slot you think is most likely to be good for the doctor."

"What a beautiful cube steak. Would you mind running it through the tenderizer a couple more times? I want my wife to be impressed with my cooking."

Ask for exactly what you want, give a reason, and offer to pay extra if necessary.

Offering to pay extra may seem like an invitation to be

taken. In practice, servers are often so pleasantly surprised that you are not going to attempt to bully them into a freebie, you get one!

"I know you normally sell these in sets. But I need only one and wouldn't mind paying a little extra if you can help me out."

"I promised my boss I would get these duplicated but forgot and left them in my car. Can I pay a little extra and get them out by this afternoon?"

Asking for good service is probably most important in a restaurant. Some menus are so complicated that an inattentive guest plus a hurried server almost guarantees a foul-up.

Something as simple as a dinner order can provide up to a dozen opportunities for error. Multiply that by the number of guests at your table, add in the other guests in the server's station, and it's downright amazing when you think of the many times you have received flawless service.

Count the chances for error in this typical service transaction:

"Good evening. My name is Jill. Can I get you something from the bar?"

"A dry Chardonnay for me, please."

"A margarita for me."

"That's a dry Chardonnay. Bottle or glass?"

"A glass will be fine."

"And will the margarita be frozen or on the rocks . . . lime or strawberry . . . with or without salt . . . glass or a pitcher?"

"Frozen, no salt, lime, and just a glass, please."

"Great. I'll be right back to take your order."

Have you been counting? There are at least seven opportunities to err. Get picky about the exact choice of wine and you easily wind up with several more potential mistakes.

Imagine how frustrating it is to wait on an inattentive, uncooperative customer who will chew you out for the slightest oversight and probably refuse to tip because of "your" poor service.

Service is a two-way street. If you want truly great service, you have to keep your end of the bargain. Pay attention, get involved, and ask for exactly what you want.

Videographer and wonderful person Donna Bryant met her match in the "wonderful" department while taping the Napa Valley Balloon crew. In Albuquerque for the annual balloon festival, Donna was taking a holiday, spending time away from the video business to relax . . . shooting video! Donna's grandson was about to celebrate a birthday, and she was assembling footage that included birthday greetings from a number of professionals.

When the balloon crew descended from their last flight of the day, Donna was there, camera in hand, requesting a quick "Happy birthday, Colin."

"You want us to say happy birthday to your grandson?"

"Well, if you don't mind."

"Of course not. We'll sing it!"

And suddenly a chorus line of free-spirited balloonists plus a few what-the-heck onlookers assembled for a one-of-a-kind birthday greeting!

11 | Let's Be Reasonable

SERVICE people have little latitude to deviate from policy. If your approach seems just right, they may bend rules, sometimes break them, to satisfy your needs. But no matter how nice you are, you just aren't going to get much in the way of accommodation if the server is likely to be penalized for going too far.

Worse, pressuring a server to do something outright impossible is as effective as beating your head against a brick wall. In fact, pushing a service person to do the impossible is the rough equivalent of beating their head against the wall.

People who deal with the public are surprisingly tolerant, but push beyond the bounds of reasonableness and you are likely to be served up a small slice of customer hell. Irritate a server and not only will you not get that extra mile of service you want, you'll be lucky if you aren't left sitting until the next shift comes on duty.

There are several ways to be unreasonable:

- Remove incentive.
- Demand an unfair share of attention.
- Demand the impossible.

Removing Incentive

Many service people are paid on commission or work for tips. Usually this can be made to work for the savvy consumer. (We'll see exactly how later.) The key point to remember: The server sees you, the consumer, as a chance to be rewarded. Remove the reward and you become a no-nentity.

For example, you are buying a car stereo system. In many shops salespersons make commissions on profit dollars: the difference between dealer cost and the sales price. That difference is often referred to as the "room to deal." Plenty of room exists in a high-profit sale.

When commissions are structured this way, both the dealer and the salesperson have an interest in making the sale with as little discounting as possible, but they don't want to be so inflexible that the customer walks. Successful operations have a record of high-profit sales as well as a high rate of close: the percentage of customers who actually purchase.

While many consumers don't know that they can negotiate a better price, others make it a point of personal pride to "beat up on" salespeople. The former get taken; the latter get no service.

The smart consumer will not take advantage of a hungry salesperson and beat them out of all their profit-dollar commission. But smart consumers do take advantage; smart consumers leave salespersons with a face-saving amount of profit and turn the potential last extra dollars of profit into service, often worth much more.

When you've bargained for a fair price, switch tactics and bargain for service. Bargaining for service is a smart move. Service can be delivered for far less than its retail value. So instead of bargaining for another fifty dollars off the sales price, let the price stand and bargain for service that would cost fifty dollars retail but that the dealer can deliver at a cost of less than ten dollars. You get fifty dollars in value, yet the dealer is out only a few bucks.

For now, realize that removing incentive is a form of unreasonable customership.

Demanding an Unfair Share of Attention

Demand more than your share of attention and the reaction you get will be on two levels.

One will be the silent reaction of a server who may not be able to give you the attention you want. The other will be the slow burn we all feel when another customer seems to be unreasonably hogging the scarce resource of personal attention.

Sure, you can bully your way to special attention. But it will have an unpleasant tension to it that detracts from its value. The best attention of all? When people knock themselves out to serve you because of who you are, not what you are or what negative consequences you threaten.

Demanding the Impossible

What is or is not possible often has little or no relationship to reality. Properly motivated servers are frequently able to do the impossible. They can find a seat on an airline that according to the computer does not exist, or discover that the part you need won't have to be ordered after all.

I once ordered a beer in a Chinese restaurant that did not have a liquor license. Because I was nice, a waiter, on his own initiative, went out into the rainy night to make a special purchase, suddenly appearing at my table with the beer.

The impossible sometimes seems possible when a room is found in a fully booked hotel or emergency alterations are performed even though no tailor is on duty. Still, there are times when customers request service that just cannot be done.

A small-town restaurateur experienced difficulties with his soda equipment on a busy holiday weekend. His frustration boiled over when his repeated attempts to contact the service department failed.

When he was finally able to connect, he indulged in several minutes of time-wasting harangue before demanding that he receive immediate attention.

"I want you to fix my equipment personally," he shouted. "And you had darn well better be here in thirty minutes if not sooner. You can also expect that Monday I'll be switching my account to your competitor." With that, he slammed the phone into its cradle.

Think about it. The owner demanded that the service manager personally fix his equipment. He demanded a thirty-minute response time from a man working nearly sixty miles away. Worst of all, he promised to switch to the competition anyway.

How do you think the problem was resolved?

Now think of how the story might have unfolded if the restaurateur had been a more savvy consumer.

"This is Able in Fredericksburg, and am I glad to hear your voice!"

"Sorry, we are absolutely swamped. I've been handling service calls myself just to try to catch up. What's your situation?"

"We're getting clobbered and our drink system is completely out. We're serving canned sodas, but you know what that's doing to profits. Can you help me?"

"First, let me see if we can diagnose this by phone. If that doesn't work, I'll call your route man at home and see if we can get you some free product to tide you over until I can spring one of my people loose. The travel time is a problem for us today. With so many calls, we can help three or four local folks in the time it takes us to get to you and back."

"Well, if you can get product here and I don't end up losing my shirt, I'll be happy to wait until you can get someone here.

Better yet, if you would like to take your family for a nice ride in the country after work, I'll spring for dinner."

People really will bend over backward when they can. Not demanding the impossible has a way of helping people whose service you need. Look for possible solutions that fall outside the norm.

12 | The Art of Tipping

JIM CONLAN works for M & M/Mars Candy Company. He understands the principles of leverage.

You could say that Jim is a nice guy.

You could also say that he is a manipulator.

Maybe we'll settle on "nice manipulator."

Perhaps you have discovered that this book is about manipulating people. Doesn't sound too nice, does it? Well, there are all sorts of ways to manipulate people, to get them to do your bidding. Brainwashing is one method. A gun works nicely in some instances.

Basically, there are two approaches to manipulation. One is positive, the way Jim Conlan does it. The other is negative, the cattle-prod method.

Jim rewards people for good behavior. He's a master at the art of tipping. Here's a "typical Conlan" example:

Jim frequents the White House, a small hotel in Chicago. It's not one of those megaproperties where you need public transit to get from your room to the lobby. The White House is small, even intimate.

Jim understands that to get Positively Outrageous Service

you have to know and be known by those who serve you. At a small place like the White House, truly personal service is possible.

Simply frequenting smaller establishments does not, of course, guarantee personal service. It only makes it more likely. You, the customer, patron, or guest, must keep your half of the bargain by being approachable and by shrewdly marketing yourself as someone worthy of special attention.

Jim does all this and more.

When Jim arrives at the White House, he begins his stay by tipping the valet and the concierge. Jim has a busy schedule when he is on the road. He often carries samples and marketing materials. This means frequent in-and-out trips to and from his room, often carrying packages of various sizes.

For most folks this would be quite a haul. Not so for Jim. When he tips the valet and concierge, he tells them that it is "only the first installment of your tip. I'll be here a few days, and I appreciate your looking out for me."

On cold mornings, Jim often heads for his rental car and finds that it is already up front, running and with the heater warming the interior. Imagine that! Someone has anticipated his needs (as well as the second installment of what promises to be a generous gratuity).

Many times when Jim returns to the hotel to change clothes, check messages, or pick up additional materials, the valet waves him into a front spot. No need to check in the car or pay an additional fee.

"Put it right next to the building, Mr. Conlan. I'll keep an eye on it!"

Jim expects and gets similar service from the concierge.

When all is said and done, Jim may spend less, certainly no more, than if he paid for in-and-out parking and tipped even modestly every time he needed special-attention service. Better yet, Jim gets honored-guest treatment because his servers are told right up front that good service is both rewarded and appreciated.

Looking at the mechanics of tipping the Conlan way, we see these principles at work:

- Tip in advance.
- Tip generously.
- Tip proportionately.

Tip in Advance

Tipping in advance is a smart move — not the entire tip, just the first installment. It puts the server on notice that you put a premium on service, or at least that, unlike some tightfisted customers, you do tip.

Waiting until the transaction is complete to slide a gratuity under the edge of the plate may be good manners, but it's lousy psychology. That's because a tip, properly given, can serve three purposes.

First, tipping rewards good service. Second, tipping in advance encourages good service; it rewards anticipated good service. Third, a generous tip positions you for fabulous service on your next visit.

In our small town we have a fantastic restaurant, the Cowboy Steakhouse. It's not the prettiest place in the world, but the steaks melt in your mouth and the desserts are from just this side of heaven. We always ask to be seated in Nancy's station, we always give Nancy a big tip, and we always get fabulous service.

What makes our visit interesting? We own a fast-food restaurant that specializes in fried chicken. Now, what do you suppose I always order at the Cowboy Steakhouse? Why, chicken, of course! Lorrie, one of the owners, always greets me with a hug and immediately begins to tease me about ordering chicken.

Naturally, she explains to her other customers that we own a chicken restaurant — and look where I eat chicken! I good-humoredly tell everyone within earshot to order the chicken.

Some time ago, on a hot, dusty summer evening, I did my usual routine when asked what I wanted to drink. Moving my hands and arms in an arc wide enough to describe a fifty-five-gallon barrel, I said, "Bring me a small glass of water." Nancy smiled and retreated to the bar. Within seconds, Nancy and Lorrie were parading back to our table with a margarita glass that must have held a gallon. It took two hands to manipulate that monster, but I didn't run out of water. And no one ran out of fun.

Tip Generously

Tipping makes a point. A large tip says that the service was appreciated and that you are generous. No tip at all says that you are cheap.

Tip Proportionately

Poor service can be blamed almost entirely on two causes: dumb management and stupid customers.

We've already talked about how management designs jobs so that servers have limited power when it comes to making service decisions. Worse, management seems quick to take a bow when things go well, but woe unto the poor server who makes a decision that flops.

If you thought you could get clobbered for straying from policy, just how flexible would you be?

Even though dumb managers make poor service inevitable, stupid customers perpetuate it. The behavior you get is always the behavior you reward. In today's economy, thousands of businesses fail each year. There should be more!

In a democratic economy, consumers vote at the cash register. Stupid customers keep voting for businesses that deserve to die. They keep poor selection, low quality, and lousy service alive by returning time after time for more abuse.

Tipped employees are often rewarded for the worst of service.

"Oh, I just couldn't walk out without leaving a little something. They have bills to pay too!"

Nice going! Leave a tip for rotten service and you encourage more rotten service. When you get poor service, what's the nicest thing you could do? Don't leave a tip, and explain why. Sometimes that second step is difficult. Well, difficult or not, it needs to be taken.

"It's not my job to train someone else's employees," you may explain. Not true. Every time you leave a tip you train. You reward a repeat performance of the service you just received. If you tipped for good service, the employee is rewarded and will probably repeat the behavior. If you reward poor service, why should you be surprised if you get more of the same?

If you want to make a statement, you can make a powerful one with a small tip. A one-penny tip boldly states, "This service stinks." Ask servers how they react to a penny tip and almost all of them will say, "It makes me think about what I did to offend my guest."

One fellow who doesn't feel comfortable verbally explaining a small tip — or none at all — leaves a card that reads:

> My tip would have been larger
> if my service had been better —
> so here is a tip for you —
> fast, friendly, accurate service
> results in better tips.

As an alternative, why not write a short note on the guest check, such as: "Service was slow and not very friendly." They will get the message.

How much is enough?

It has never made much sense to tip a fixed percentage of the check. After all, how much more effort is required to serve an expensive steak than a sandwich? There may be some difference, but how much?

Does someone who serves a $5.99 blue plate special work half as hard as someone serving an $11.95 entrée? Probably not. Strictly based on percentages, a 25 percent tip may be just right for the former, 15 percent for the latter.

Base your tip decision solely on the service provided. Give weight to the skill required, the degree of difficulty, and perhaps the ability of the server to earn tips over the period of their shift.

Friendly service, maybe with a little appropriate conversation tossed in, should receive a better reward than service that is no more than politely efficient.

Extra points go to servers who notice or anticipate special needs: bringing crackers for the baby or offering a helpful suggestion on those days when you can't seem to make up your mind.

Service that requires special training or knowledge should be rewarded, such as helping with a lobster shell or a knowledgeable suggestion for the wine selection.

In theme restaurants, servers participate in the entertainment. If you enjoyed the entertainment, pay the piper.

A group of business associates decided to end a long day at a restaurant called the Bombay Bicycle Club. When their server noticed that they were more interested in relaxing than in deciding what to order, he took control of their entire evening.

Stuffing oranges into his apron top, he announced that he thought the group would be better served by "Mom." Everyone was told to relax and let Mom take care of everything. With that, he selected an entrée that he thought each person would enjoy.

During the meal, he stopped frequently to entertain his guests, explaining at one stop that in real life he performed as a comedian. No doubt!

At the end of the evening, he wheeled out a brass cart laden with ice cream and other dessert items and proceeded to concoct custom desserts for the delighted diners.

What do you think would have been an appropriate tip? Ten percent? Fifteen? Twenty? The correct answer is "none of the above." Positively Outrageous Service should not be rewarded according to some calculator total. Reward Positively Outrageous Service with an equally outrageous tip.

How to Tip

It's okay to be discreet, but a tip slid under the plate as you leave deprives you of the opportunity to be personally connected to the tip. When you tip, look the server directly in the eye and say exactly why you are so pleased:

"Thank you for your good service, Martha. I always appreciate it when people remember the little details of my order. And I especially like not having to go looking for a refill of my water."

Now you have a server who knows exactly what you want and that when you get it you are likely to tip generously. To make the transaction complete, you remembered to use her name, a perfect touch.

To make the whole event memorable, pause briefly on your way out and tell the manager, "That Martha is terrific! The best service I've had anywhere. She deserves a pat on the back."

If the manager is not visible, comment to the host or hostess, "Good night, and thank you for seating me in Martha's station. She was great."

To get the maximum payback on tipping, ask to be waited on by the same server on your next visit. Talk about feeling special — when you return and ask to be seated in Martha's station, you will have a friend for life.

Tipping generously is nice, but praising generously is more important.

The No-Tip Tip

A tip doesn't have to be cash. Effective tips are often no more than a kind word or, in some cases, a clever word.

We were trying to hurry through the supermarket one busy Saturday and were doing fine until it came time to check out. All lanes were open and full, so I cruised the registers until I found the checker with the most signs of life out of a crew that gave the appearances of having been rode hard and put up wet (a horse term, for you city folks).

Walking to the front of the line, I leaned close and said, "We've been watching you, and you are really fast!"

I smiled, returned to my place in line, and enjoyed the show as our checker put on quite a display just to prove my point.

13 | Tell Everyone

CONSUMERS never hesitate to spread the news about bad service. Not that you shouldn't warn your friends, it's just that too often we talk to everyone but the person who could change the situation. Worse than that is the fact that we do not put nearly as much effort into spreading good news.

The best tip you can leave in any operation (it doesn't have to be a restaurant) is to tell the world when the product and service has been wonderful.

If you get truly outstanding service, take a few minutes to write a short note or letter. This is actually smart shopping on your part, because it absolutely guarantees that on your next visit you will be treated like royalty.

When folks know you're going to report them, they go nuts trying to be perfect. One-Eyed Jack, the fast-talking DJ for WMAY in Springfield, Illinois, is the terror of the town with his Lightning Lunch Awards. He likes to visit fast-food eateries and time the service at the drive-through. He reports the results on his show. Jack told me that drive-through customers report record fast service when they mention his name as they place their order!

Lightning Lunch Awards are fun, but they tend to emphasize the negative. Here's how we use the positive power of reporting on performance:

We have a driver from McLane Foodservice who apparently missed the training session where drivers are taught advanced annoyance, rudeness, and laziness. Tom, our driver, gets special treatment from us. He can deliver anytime he pleases. Why? Because he always asks in a way that lets you know that if he must wait, he will do so gladly. If a delivery is short, he is the first to point out the error. Best of all, Tom does more than drop product. He puts the product right onto the shelves, even taking the time to rotate the goods so that older product is up front, where it will be used first.

In December, an especially busy month, we took a few minutes to write a nice letter to Tom's boss. A few days later, a beaming driver showed up and couldn't wait to tell about being called into the president's office. He thought he must have done something awful to warrant attention from the big boss.

Imagine his surprise and relief when, instead of a reprimand, he received a personal thank you, a copy of our letter, and was told that a record of the event would go into his personnel file.

Now look at this from our point of view. We already got great service from Tom, but taking the time to say thanks — all the way to the top — pretty much guarantees that when we need a little extra attention, Tom will see that we get it.

Saying thank you all the way to the top is more than a good tip for good service. It's the best insurance you can have that future service will also be wonderful.

Besides telling the boss, go the extra mile and tell another customer or potential customer.

"If you are unhappy with your service, please tell us.
If you enjoyed your service, please tell everybody!"

Since writing my first book, *Positively Outrageous Service,* I've received letters from people all over the country telling me their favorite service stories. Here are a few. Some will make you smile, and others will make you shake your head in disbelief.

Dan Newbould bought a new Sable from Middlecroft Mercury in Salt Lake City. Dan loved the car, even though it had a minor bug in the brake system that took three visits to cure. Dan didn't mind because the folks at Middlecroft did so much to make up for the inconvenience.

Each time Dan pulled into their drive, an alert clerk entered his license into a computer, enabling the service manager to greet Dan by name. Dan's car was always washed and vacuumed prior to pickup. Makes you want to stop in at Middlecroft Mercury and buy a new Sable . . . or at least complain about your brakes!

At Cooper 5 Theatres in Denver, Bill Welch and crew were testing the interlock system, a mechanical hookup that allows theaters to show one print of a film in two auditoriums, more or less at the same time.

Since it was midday, one of the auditoriums was closed. Then an employee spotted a birthday party of ten young boys. Quick-thinking Bill had them ushered into the closed auditorium for their own showing.

Melium Potash of Sandburg Supermarkets reports that when a customer has a baby, they send a fruit basket, an album of clippings from the newspaper on the day the baby was born, a bib, and a circular announcing the birth.

A Page Avjet employee tells of entering an auto parts store only to discover that even though he was the only customer, the clerk refused to serve him until he had taken a number. The clerk apparently felt better knowing that events were occurring in the proper order.

Linda Fort of the Y-O Ranch Hilton encountered a one-of-a-kind situation when a visiting two-bus tour group of Belgian butchers came close to a riot. One bus carried Flemish-speaking butchers, the other French-speaking butchers. The two groups mixed about as well as oil and water. To the tour operator's dismay, they expected the tour to include visits to packing plants and slaughterhouses.

(I couldn't make up a story like this.)

By the time the group reached the Y-O in Kerrville, Texas, they were at each other's throats.

Linda called Mike Hughes, who owns Texas Wild Game Co-op, at 8 A.M. the next day and said, "Mike, I need your help! Can I send ninety people who don't speak English and hate each other out to your packing plant in one hour? They're butchers from Belgium, and they want to see some blood and guts."

Mike said, "Sure! Send them on out."

That visit saved the rest of their tour in Texas.

In Madison, Wisconsin, Dane County Credit Union president Linda Wilkinson spent an afternoon washing windshields and chattering with members to help inaugurate the newly expanded drive-up.

Check my balance . . . and add a quart of oil!

On the train from Grand Central Terminal in Manhattan to Norwalk, Connecticut, I heard this PA announcement: "(Cough, cough, cough, cough) No smoking, please!"

This was followed by the appearance of a smiling conductor who sang, "Watch your step. Watch your step. Be ready with your tickets. Be ready to move. Just be ready!"

Next up was a detailed three-day weather forecast, a reminder of the change to daylight savings time, and a wish for us all to have a pleasant weekend.

Who says New Yorkers are rude and pushy?

You can't please everyone. The owner of an auto repair shop went the extra mile and repaired a gear shift for a customer at no charge after it fell off as they were moving the vehicle into the garage.

Who would have expected the customer to become irate and yell, "Put it back just the way you found it! That was my burglar alarm. I pull it out and take it into the house at night!"

At the Dairy Queen in Gregory, Texas, a sure bet for friendly service, one of the owners was startled to find a customer sitting on a chair in the walk-in cooler.

"She looked like she was about to have a heat stroke," explained an employee. "So we put her in there to cool her off!"

My gran greeted her neighbor, Bill, and asked where he'd been.

"I went to visit an old school chum that I haven't seen in over forty years."

"Did he recognize you, Bill?"

"He didn't even open his eyes. He was at the funeral parlor."

(Okay, so it's not a service story. But it's true, and I thought you'd enjoy it!)

Looking for a place to eat dinner in Campbell River, British Columbia, Canada, Melanie and I stepped into the last unlocked shop on the main street. It was a trophy and engraving shop. The owner, who was working late, recommended Painter's Cove, on the edge of town.

"Thanks," we said, and stepped out the door, intending to walk.

"Wait just a minute!" she shouted, grabbing her purse and

running for the door. "It's much too far to walk. I'll drive you."

If you're ever in Campbell River, buy a trophy!

Daphne DeMaris recommends Domino's Pizza. Friends of Daphne's decided to eat at a competing pizza restaurant. After a very long wait to order, they were told that the restaurant was out of the ingredients for the pizza of their choice. They had to settle for another variety. One of the guests, out of frustration, if not spite, called Domino's and persuaded them to deliver to the restaurant. Domino's managed to deliver exactly their order before the other pizza was ready.

The diners wrote letters to both pizza chains, just to see what would happen. The first chain sent a letter of lame excuse and a coupon good for ten dollars off on the next visit. The Domino's people sent a letter of thanks and coupons worth twenty dollars!

14 Roll into Position for the Next Shot

GOOD POOL players know that a great shot does more than put the right ball in the right pocket: A great shot rolls into position for a great follow-up shot. A good player makes one shot at a time. A great player plans ahead. Instead of making one good shot and looking helpless, great players plan ahead and often run the table. They just look lucky.

The same can be said of smart consumers. They market themselves to get the most of their current buying experience, but they also plant subtle seeds that ensure that the next visit will be equally pleasant and productive.

Smart consumers:

- Establish personal relationships.
- Anticipate future quality or service problems.
- Shape expectations for future transactions.

Establish Personal Relationships

The first relationship to establish — call it loyalty — is with the individual mechanic, ticket agent, stylist, or whoever will actually deliver the service you need. Servers love to be asked for by name, especially by an appreciative, easy-to-deal-with customer.

Earlier we learned that one sure step to better service is to deny anonymity to the server. Beyond denying anonymity, develop a personal relationship. Knowing a little something about a regular server's family, tastes, or hobbies often establishes a common bond.

Why do you think strangers often talk about the weather or sports? It's to start a conversation through a subject that both parties are likely to have in common. From there, little verbal clues point the way toward less ordinary topics. When all is said and done, good service resembles pleasant conversation. Each party — emphasis here on "each" — anticipates the needs of the other.

This may not sit particularly well with those folks who say, "I pay enough for good service that I shouldn't have to work at it." First, getting good service does not require work so much as it requires participation. Second, there's a difference between service performed grudgingly and service that springs from an honest desire to please. Which would you prefer?

To establish personal relationships, first confer loyalty. When you get good, efficient service from someone, make it a point to ask for their name. Then, on the next visit, ask for that server. This automatically improves your odds of a repeat, positive performance.

Over time, you won't be able to avoid learning little tidbits about your server — small things, like a birthday, a grandchild who likes stuffed rabbits, a friend who lives in Omaha. Then, in the ordinary course of living, you will be able to match odd pieces of information to your benefit.

Thoughtfulness is a subtle way to remind people that you recognize their humanity. Too often the customer-server relationship is looked upon as a master-slave contract. But that doesn't get you Positively Outrageous Service.

Several years ago Mary, who had been my travel agent for

years, decided to marry and move away. I asked her to introduce me to someone in her office she could recommend to
handle my business. Then I sent her flowers.

Nancy was Mary's designated successor for my business.
Nancy had to feel special, because Mary had handpicked her,
even taking the time to introduce us by phone. The flowers
were the finishing touch — not only a nice way to say a sincere
thank you to Mary, they let the rest of the office staff know
that at least one customer recognized and appreciated great
service.

The relationship was further cemented later when the
agency manager enclosed a service questionnaire with my
tickets. The questionnaire covered all the usual points of service. Just to keep things in perspective, I wrote at the bottom
of the form: "Nancy is my personal travel agent. She knows me
and she delivers exactly the service I like. Your agency is fine,
but if Nancy goes . . . so do I!"

Establish one other great relationship — with the owner or
manager. Not that you should expect special favors, but sometimes a little inside pull helps. At a minimum, the staff's
knowledge of that relationship will prevent any outright poor
service. Beyond that, knowing the manager could get you a
table, a price break, extended hours, extra service, or an inside tip.

Anticipate Future Quality
or Service Problems

Solve quality or service problems before they occur.
If it's a big-ticket item, you'll want to get promises in writing,
especially if repairs or replacement could be difficult or expensive.

For small items, a simple mention of your concern may be
all that's needed to smooth the way in the event that you must
return to set things right. For example, you spot a sale item
that would be perfect for a friend's birthday. You're fairly sure

of the size but not absolutely certain. Could you get a refund if it doesn't fit? The simple solution: Ask.

"I notice that your sign says no refunds or exchanges on sale items from this rack. I would like to buy this for a friend's birthday, and I'm fairly sure the size is correct. But what if it isn't?"

Most of the time you'll get the answer you want. To be sure the situation won't change by the time you return, get approval from someone likely to be around and in authority.

Anticipating future quality or service problems is really a matter of asking for some type of guarantee, whether it's written or verbal. Big-ticket items should never be purchased from temporary outlets or deep-discounters. Unless the product comes with an ironclad factory warranty, you're asking for trouble.

Shape Expectations for Future Transactions

As you walk out the door, always try to do something that telegraphs your expectation for future transactions. Something as simple as "I really appreciate how you always find us a table with a view" plants two thoughts: that you have enjoyed and appreciate the service just received and that you anticipate a repeat performance.

We attended an association dinner meeting held in a private dining room at the Cowboy Steakhouse. The menu that evening was sirloin tips, but I was served a wonderful mesquite-broiled breast of chicken. I didn't have to ask; it just appeared. (Remember in an earlier chapter how I *always* eat chicken at their steakhouse? They remembered!)

Good Customers Are Valuable

Being a good customer will ensure that when you need service, even if it's something special, you'll get it.

Why are good customers valued? Because they ask for exactly what they want, thus making service fun and easy. No mystery. No surprises. And good customers reward good service. One way is by paying promptly.

Do you think prompt payment is important?

Read this letter we received from one of our maintenance contractors:

Dear Scott and Melanie,

In looking through my records, I found that you have been very prompt with payments. Some payments have been received within a week of the day the services were performed. I would like to take a moment to thank you, and tell you how much that is appreciated.

This is a sign to me that you appreciate my service and respect my business, and I thank you for that. I will make sure your service needs are met promptly and in the most economical way possible. I hope to continue to serve you, and again I thank you very much for being such a good customer.

Sincerely,
Lee Tenery

Roll into position for the next shot. Pave the way for great service by being a great customer.

15 | Support Your Local . . .

PRICE means nothing without service. Customers who make price the sole factor in their buying decisions are making a terrible mistake.

Wiley Rains supplies our cole slaw mix. It's not cheap, but it is the best — and if we run short, we can call Wiley at home.

Moe and Linn supply our computer hardware and software. Catalogue dealers are cheaper, but they won't come to my house on weekends to solve problems.

Ignore the small-business owner and shop exclusively at the discount house, but don't come crying when you have a question or need someone to sponsor the little league and discover that the little guy is out of business. You did it.

Price is important, but weigh other factors, too.

The mother of my friend George Samaras was hospitalized. A beautiful woman, she was concerned when her hairdo showed the inevitable signs of a prolonged hospital stay. Eva, her beautician of many years, made the thirty-five-mile drive to the hospital, performed her miracle, and charged not a single penny.

Try getting service like that from some take-a-number-please salon.

One day Vance and Betty Coleman, regular customers at Ed Marlatt's Church's Chicken restaurant in San Antonio, did not show up for their daily lunch. Because the couple are in their eighties, the manager called, and learned that the person who usually gave them a ride had been called away on a trip. The manager immediately delivered their usual order to their home and told them that someone from Church's would call to check every morning until their friend returned. The employees even made plans to take them grocery shopping. It's no wonder that Vance and Betty refer to them as family!

Smart customers do business where they are recognized as individuals. The only places this can happen are businesses that treat employees like something more than cattle.

Mom walked in this morning with a bag of fresh, still-warm baked goodies. She also brought a story.

At the bakeshop, a new employee had prepared a fresh pot of coffee. She remembered the filter. She remembered the ground coffee. She remembered to press the start button. She forgot the pot.

A shouted warning from a customer enabled her to quickly put an empty pot in place. With a smile and a shrug, she gave the waiting customers a body-language sign that communicated her embarrassment. ("I did it again!")

Just then the owner walked out from the back.

"Well, she did it again," a nearby customer chided.

"Looks like you're going to have to fire the new kid," chimed in another.

The owner frowned and raised a wrinkled brow as if to say "Not a bad idea" before huffing into the back again.

"You never see many of the same faces twice," Mom continued. "It must not be a very pleasant place to work."

If employees are hired to serve customers, what then is the job of management? To serve the employees. Management serves by providing training, tools, and other forms of physical, financial, and emotional support.

Unsupported employees cannot provide good service. And so they leave.

Smart customers understand that a stable work force is a sign of good service. Smart customers never do business where a help-wanted sign is in the window. What better sign that your chances of getting good service are slim to none?

Not only should you attempt to be a regular, loyal customer, you should make it a point to do business where the employees have been around longer than the soap in the restroom.

We visited Macaroni's Bar and Grill in Dallas for the first time, accompanied by two business associates.

"Hi! I'm Chris," was the cheerful greeting offered by our server.

"Hi! I'm Scott, and this is Larry, Curly, and Moe."

"Can I get you something from the bar, or would you like to order?"

"Yes and yes. We're in a bit of a hurry, so can you take the entire order at once?"

"Sure."

We ordered, and Chris headed for the kitchen. Then he hesitated and turned, saying, "Are you their boss?"

"Why? Do you think I should be?"

"Actually, I wouldn't mind having you for a boss, but I don't think you are."

"Why?"

"Too jovial!"

Customers tend to be lazy — and cheap! They do business without thinking in advance about such issues as quality service and guarantees. Instead, they do business with the least-expensive or most-convenient supplier. Sometimes this is the right decision. Too often it's a horrible mistake.

Customers should shop first for the vendor and second for the item. You may pay a few cents more on any particular item, but in the long run you'll save money, time, and frustration.

Mom and Pop

Large or small, independent or chain, every business is a Mom-and-Pop operation. Somebody's Mom or Pop is in charge.

Mom and Pop can provide superior personal service. A free-lance editor in New York City frequently gets packages delivered by messenger. The messengers are told to deliver to him at home, "or to Frank, at the drugstore across the street." Frank, the pharmacist, also cashes the occasional check when the editor runs short over the weekend.

Though there are many delightful exceptions, huge chain stores are not places where you would expect above-and-beyond service. In huge stores employees see so many customers that they all become just another face in a sea of faces. Still, not all exceptional servers own their own business or work in a small shop shoulder-to-shoulder with a caring, supportive boss. Here's a case in point:

A San Antonio attorney waited too long to buy a toy that his young son wanted for Christmas. By the time the attorney found time to shop, the toy had completely disappeared from local toy store shelves.

He called up major stores in surrounding cities and towns. Always he got the same response: "Sorry, sold out."

Then he reached the manager of a Wal-Mart nearly 150 miles away. The manager, who could easily sell the high-demand toy locally, asked for the boy's name and address and the attorney's credit card number.

In a few days, a package arrived, wrapped in brown paper. In the rush of Christmas, it was left untouched until Christmas Eve. As the attorney and his wife were placing packages under the tree and wrapping last-minute gifts, they tore the brown paper off the package. Inside was the toy, beautifully wrapped in Santa Claus paper. On top was a handwritten card from the Wal-Mart manager to their son. It explained that St. Nick had left the package at Wal-Mart by mistake and had asked that it be sent to its new owner.

Inside the card was a picture of Santa himself.

Proof in point that good people, friendly people, can be found anywhere. When customers explain their problems and, in a pleasant, vulnerable manner, ask for help, small miracles are more than just possible. They actually happen. Even for attorneys!

After a radio interview, a nice gentleman called our office to order two copies of *Positively Outrageous Service*, for Christmas presents. We took his name, address, and credit card information, and in hours his order was in the mail.

Unfortunately, the zip code on the package was incorrect. A few days before Christmas the customer called to say that the books had not arrived.

In minutes, two autographed copies, posted for special delivery on Christmas Day, were on their way, at no extra charge.

The job left for the customer who experiences this Positively Outrageous Service is to tell everyone who will listen and to pledge their future business. This keeps the doors open when competition strikes with lower prices or some other temporary advantage.

Even the post office, the ultimate monopoly and much-bashed bastion of rules and bureaucracy, can be an outstanding example of service and value. Complain if you will, but think for a moment how inexpensive it is to send a letter, often thousands of miles to the least-accessible reaches of the planet.

One such "inaccessible reach" is our home town of Center Point, Texas, a place so small we don't even have a town drunk. (We take turns.) The Center Point post office closes promptly at 4:30 P.M. Unless, of course, you ask.

The other day a client called at 4:25 with an emergency need for next-day delivery of documents. Too late for Federal Express and miles from possible air freight, we raced to the post office, only to arrive at 4:31.

No problem — my wife had phoned ahead. A hand beckoned from a side entrance. The postmistress herself offered an Overnight Mail envelope and saved both my day and my client.

It's not likely that a customer who had not taken the time to establish a relationship would get that kind of service.

Recognizing Good Service Providers

According to *Fortune* magazine, America's ten most-admired companies are Merck Pharmaceuticals, Rubbermaid, Wal-Mart, Liz Claiborne, Levi-Strauss, Johnson & Johnson, Coca-Cola, 3M, Pepsico, and Procter & Gamble.

Fortune considered these key attributes: quality of management; quality of products and service; ability to attract, develop, and keep talented people; innovativeness; community and environmental responsibility.

The *Fortune* list shows great service providers. Here's a slightly expanded list of attributes, aimed at the individual consumer:

- A no-hassle returns policy.
- Satisfaction guaranteed.
- People who care.
- Convenient hours.
- Choice of delivery systems.
- An order system that is easy to understand and use.
- Fair, though not necessarily lowest, prices.

- Fanatic concern over product safety and quality.
- Knowledgeable staff.
- An easily accessible system for conflict resolution.

Also, although it may not directly affect the speed or quality of the service you receive, I think that it's a sign of concern and integrity when a business makes a special effort to hire the handicapped. Let's talk about a few of these.

No-hassle returns policy

"If you are unsatisfied for any reason, simply return your merchandise for replacement or a full refund."

In twenty-five words or less, that's the kind of guarantee that you should seek. Notice the key words: "for any reason," "replacement," "full refund." Unfortunately, too many companies add stipulations such as "with receipt," "within thirty days," and "with original packaging."

Sears may have the most famous guarantee. If a Craftsman hand tool ever breaks or fails to perform for any reason, simply return it for a quick, friendly, no-questions-asked replacement.

Another great guarantee accompanied the introduction of the new Saturn automobile line, produced by GM. Buyers were given the option of returning any car within thirty days of purchase, no questions asked, for a complete refund, regardless of miles driven or mechanical condition.

Satisfaction guaranteed

Hampton Inn was first on the guarantee bandwagon in the lodging industry. They said, "If you have a problem or complaint at any time during your stay and are not satisfied when you leave, we'll give you one night's stay for free."

Ray Schultz, president and chief executive officer of Hampton Inns, explained in the *Wall Street Journal,*

". . . I wondered how we could be sure that every air conditioner was working, every carpet was clean and every bed was freshly made in each of our 23,000 rooms. I worried that our new employees might not share the sense of motivation our original team had. And I worried that a slip in our standards would send unhappy guests somewhere else.

"To maintain the quality of our service we began devising employee retention strategies. We also looked at proposals for building customer loyalty. But rather than devising a complex mixture of strategies to satisfy these two concerns, we discovered that the solution to both challenges lay in a single promise . . . an unconditional 100 percent satisfaction guarantee."

About 99 percent of the guests who invoke the guarantee come back. In fact, after perfect service the first time around, guests (customers) like knowing that they can rely on their hosts to set things right.

Guarantees aren't limited to hotels and frypans. Richard B. Chase, a professor at the business school of the University of Southern California, decided that professors should practice what they teach. He guarantees to students that if they aren't satisfied with the way he taught, he will pay for their books plus $250 toward class fees.

The superstars bet their bottom line on products and services that satisfy. They offer guarantees that become a permanent part of their service offerings, cost structure, and corporate culture.

You can price-shop, but a superior guarantee is priceless. You may be pleased with a deep-discount deal, but see how you feel when problems arise. When it comes to guarantees, this one is stellar:

100% GUARANTEE
All of our products are guaranteed to give 100 percent satisfaction in every way. Return anything purchased

from us at any time if it proves otherwise. We will replace it, refund your purchase price or credit your credit card, as you wish. We do not want you to have anything from L.L. Bean that is not completely satisfactory.

For the best of the best, service guarantees become part of a long-term, winning tradition, as this story from Red Lobster demonstrates:

Two business people were enjoying lunch at a Red Lobster restaurant. The service was fast and friendly, and their lunch was excellent. They were completely surprised when a manager approached their table, signed their guest check, and apologized for a lunch that had taken all of eleven minutes to serve.

"Sorry it took longer than our guaranteed time of ten minutes. Lunch is on us today. Please give us another try soon."

People who care

The best way to tell if a business is people-friendly: Step inside the door and take a psychological inventory of the people they employ. Employees mirror management.

Just as individuals have distinct personalities, any organization has a personality that is the collective average of the personalities of its members.

Love, Mickey

A friend tells the story of his visit to Disneyland. He and his wife had saved pennies to be able to take their two children on a once-in-a-lifetime vacation. Of course, to the little ones Mickey Mouse was the center of all conversation and attention.

On the last day, with his kids still touring the Magic Kingdom, my friend checked out of the hotel. As the bellhop loaded the bags into the station wagon, my friend told him how the kids had adored their time at "Mickey's house."

The bellhop whipped out a pen and notepad, leaving this cheerful note to delight and surprise the children:

"Thanks for visiting my Magic Kingdom. Love, Mickey."

Mom delivers

When my mother asked if she could sign on as a delivery driver at our restaurant, I wasn't certain how to respond. It's tough work, the hours are long, and our drivers are expected to deliver in bad weather and to sometimes less-than-desirable areas of town.

I figured, why not just say yes and let Mom learn her own lesson. Instead, Mom taught us a lesson about service and the unconditional love that truly great service requires.

Imagine our surprise one morning, just days before Christmas, to see Mom loading her van with several brightly wrapped packages. They were bundles of slippers, each lovingly knitted by Mom and wrapped with love, presents for her favorite customers.

Mom also loves her unlovable customers — she gives them a big hello and her best service.

Convenient Hours

You shop at K mart because they are open when you are ready to buy and when you need something in hurry. K mart's hours are their competitive advantage.

You think K mart is inexpensive? That's not necessarily so. But whether or not you go there because of price, convenient shopping hours pulled you in the door the first time.

If you know of a small business where you like to shop, do them a favor by telling them every time you stop at a K mart to buy something you would have purchased at their place if they had been open.

The most glaring example of inconvenient hours may be the telephone company. But then, why not? They're a monopoly. So when you need to install a new phone and the service representative says, "We'll be out to install your phone on Wednesday," most consumers are smart enough not to bother asking, "What time Wednesday?"

I'll never forget the day I tried to order service for our new home. This was in the years when Ma Bell was queen of the universe.

To order, you had to go to the "Phone Store." The company that made such a big deal out of letting your fingers do the walking wouldn't accept telephone inquiries. You want a phone? Then you come to us.

At the Phone Store, I was approached by a young woman who informed me, "All of our sales counselors are busy."

"I don't really need counseling as much as I need telephone service. Since I'm the only one waiting, maybe you can help me."

"Sorry, sir, but it's my turn to greet the customers. You'll have to wait."

I waited . . . and waited.

Finally, my greeter escorted me to a desk for counseling, where another sharp young woman launched into a sophisticated sales pitch.

"Excuse me, ma'am. I had to take off from work to be here. We already own our phones. All I need is someone to run the wire to our new house."

After a few more minutes, we hit an impasse when she requested information I would have to go home to get.

"I'll call you with that information as soon as possible. What number should I call?"

"You'll have to come in. You can't call."

"I can't call the phone company? You should see a telephone counselor and set up a line!"

"Sorry, but that's our policy."

"You aren't telling me that you don't have a telephone. I can see them all over the office!"

"I'm just telling you that you can't call here."

I grabbed a piece of paper and scribbled the number posted on her desk phone.

"Sir, you'll have to give me that paper! That paper is the property of this telephone company. I can't let you leave here with that paper."

With that last ridiculous remark, I tore off a small section that contained the number, crumpled it, and popped it into my mouth.

"You'll never take me alive," I snarled.

The phone company, the government, and other monopolies aren't about to operate on K mart time. They've got it. No one else has it. If you want it, wait.

Smart business owners listen to their customers, discover their unfilled needs and unsolved problems, and do whatever it takes to fill those needs and solve those problems. It may mean developing a new product. The solution is usually much more simple.

David Jackson (who stars on the cover of this book) cuts my hair. My hair doesn't grow where I need it. Worse, it never needs to be cut at a convenient time.

"Hello, David. This is Scott. Do you feel like cutting hair tomorrow?"

"Sure. The afternoon is booked, but the morning is fairly open. What time would you like?"

"Afternoon. My morning is booked, and I'm also booked after three."

"What about Tuesday, first thing?"

"I'm going out of town early Tuesday. I guess it will have to wait another week, even if I do look pretty rough."

"Okay . . . Monday, nine A.M."

"That's your day off."

"I'll come in just for you."

"I'll be there. And thanks!"

To me, David Jackson is worth more because he cuts hair on Kmart time.

Hiring the handicapped

Maybe, just maybe, businesses that employ the handicapped deserve special attention from consumers. A medal may not be appropriate here but I'll tell you this: Hiring the handicapped makes a statement.

When it comes to hiring the handicapped, it's impossible to miss the fact that, other than their medical disability, handicapped folks are ordinary people. Talk to anyone who has taken a chance and hired a handicapped worker and the story you hear time and again is that handicapped workers are remarkably unremarkable.

Wanda Mitchell is our first unremarkable example. Ken Conner at Pizzeria Uno in Asheville, North Carolina, took a chance on Wanda when she was presented for employment by Handiskills, an agency that specializes in job placement for the disabled. Handiskills offered training assistance and follow-up counseling to make Wanda's entry into the work force easy for everyone.

Ken has a friend who had dealt with the Handiskills program. His friend's positive experience made it easier for Ken to say yes when Handiskills proposed Wanda for a job in the dish room.

Wanda, the victim of a serious head injury, is older than most of the crew and brings an additional sense of maturity to the staff. Wanda's crewmates say she is fun, even though she tends to be quiet and focused on the job at hand.

From an operator's viewpoint, that pretty much describes the perfect employee, doesn't it?

Add in "dependable, hard-working, and long-term" and you have a nearly unbeatable combination.

Surely there must be some kind of drawback. Ask Ken and his response is "You may have to repeat something, but other than that, she has the same problems as anyone." Excuse me. Does anyone have an employee who doesn't at least occasionally require you to repeat something?

At Pizzeria Uno, the dish room is fairly isolated from the rest of the operation. Crewmember Theresa Stills says of Wanda, "She doesn't say much. Just does her job like the rest of us." Asked if she thinks that hiring the handicapped is a good idea, Teresa matter-of-factly replies, "I don't see why not."

Teresa may not see "why not," but apparently thousands of employers haven't yet discovered the too-often-ignored value that lies untapped in minds and bodies sometimes cruelly labeled "handicapped." If Wanda Mitchell is handicapped, then maybe we all should be. Here's why:

Wanda has joined the Salvation Army and works as a volunteer Candy Striper at a hospital. Her boss rates her as average or even slightly above, and her teammates have apparently stopped seeing Wanda as different. Not a bad example for the rest of us.

His name is Jimmy. He has spent most of his life in sheltered workshops for the learning-disabled. He is strong, friendly, eager to please, and, at first meeting, very shy.

He's also my employee.

Our first meeting was in a cramped, poorly lighted, typically institutional room, more suited for interrogation than interview. I couldn't stand it, and quickly moved us into the less-confining hallway.

When we shook hands, Jimmy turned his head away completely, unable to look at me directly. But with each question he would quickly look in my direction, flash a big, winning smile, and turn away again.

His answers then, as they are today, were staccato bursts of one or two words. Jimmy must feel as if he was born with a limited supply of words. He never wastes them, and sometimes appears irritated when others do. His conversation, if you could call it that, is always meaningful, and even though it is over in only a heartbeat or so, you sense it to be warm and friendly.

Standing in the hallway, I knew that Jimmy would fit in just fine. My last question was, "Is there any time that you just can't work?"

"Mondays," was the immediate reply, the word leaping out.

"Okay, Mondays it is. If you want the job, it's yours."

"Thank you," he exploded, and this time left an extra millisecond for an extra-big smile. Then he turned and burst through the double doors to report to his peers.

"Yes!" he hissed, arms stabbing the air above him, Mary Lou Retton style. "I got the job!"

Jimmy looked like an Olympic athlete, built by nature for the wrestling team but filled with the exuberance of a gymnast. We could just barely hear his second exclamation as the doors banged shut.

"Yes! I got the job!"

For just a moment I couldn't help but feel awed at my ability to create such unbridled joy with only a few ordinary words.

Like Ken Conners, we found our experience to be extraordinarily ordinary. Jimmy is always on time. Always in uniform, clean and pressed. Always moving. Always friendly. Always.

I don't think he would do well on the cash register. He doesn't think quite fast enough to be a cook or a server. But he turned out to be a superior baker, a constant cleaner-upper, and attentive to levels of prepping items.

Unlike other handicapped employees we've had, Jimmy is not much for meeting the public. He might enjoy meeting Wanda Mitchell.

That's not to say that he cannot handle public contact. Jimmy, like anyone else, has his strengths and weaknesses. He has his own personality. His is a private soul.

That Christmas, I had a chance to get to know Jimmy a little better when I drove him home after our employee party. I didn't want to pry, but I was curious to know why he had been so quick to ask for Mondays off.

"Golf!" was his air-burst answer.

"Golf?"

"Golf!," followed by a pause to see if that would satisfy me. "I golf every Monday."

"Are you any good at it?" I asked, thinking how nice it would be to have every Monday free to do whatever I wanted.

"Sure!"

It figures.

Our first handicapped employee was Lora. Lora knew everyone in the entire Western Hemisphere. She hugged them, too. We miss seeing our guests get hugged by Lora, but she moved on to a better job with more hours and higher pay. A competitor recruited her.

Isn't that a hoot? From unemployable to highly desirable.

Once you've had the opportunity to hire a qualified handicapped person, you'll wonder what took you so long to discover this untapped source of energy and talent. When people use words like "handicapped" and "disabled," you'll know for certain that those words don't mean what they used to mean.

In fact, it hasn't been too long since those words were just plain mean. Maybe we're all growing up.

16 | We Deliver

MORE THAN ever before, delivery has become an integral part of the service. Delivery means more than home delivery. Now it's the system by which you actually receive the product or service.

Note the following examples of delivery systems and the products or services you can receive.

TELEPHONE: Consulting, information, financial transactions

MAIL: Newspapers, magazines

PARCEL POST: Retail items such as books, clothes, housewares

COMMON CARRIER: Furniture

HOME CARE: Medical, cleaning, gardening

HOME DELIVERY: Prepared food, groceries

WALK-IN: Hairstyling

DRIVE-THROUGH: Dry cleaning, food, groceries

Telephone

Some companies make it easy to place an order but difficult to solve a problem. Before you place an order via an 800 phone number, try the same number to get assistance.

Telephone shopping should give you the convenience of picking up the phone whenever it suits your schedule. In fact, greatly expanded hours and round-the-clock service are a major selling point for shopping by phone. So don't neglect to check for hours of operation before you place your catalogue order. The best will offer twenty-four-hour, seven-day service.

Only a select few extend that same great service beyond their order line. L. L. Bean stands out as the benchmark in this area, with an always-open customer service department to match their nearly flawless order department. Too often companies make it easy for you to spend but make you jump through hoops if you have a problem with your purchase.

The creators of WordPerfect, the premier word processing software, provide terrific telephone service. Unlike most software companies, WordPerfect has a toll-free number for instant, expert assistance.

My first book, *Positively Outrageous Service,* has been a hit with the business community, especially owners of small businesses. We did a nationwide media tour to talk up the book and ended up on radio and television shows in some of the most unlikely places.

The result, besides brisk sales of the book, was delightful phone conversations with call-in customers. Occasionally we'd get strange calls, like the one from a gentleman in Cincinnati who called to order the book on how to pick up girls. My wife answered that one, and I wouldn't be surprised if she gave him a couple of pointers just so he wouldn't be too disappointed over reaching the wrong number.

Other callers just had to tell us their favorite service story, and a few called to see if we were as cheerful in person as we appear in print. I don't think anyone was disappointed there!

But my favorite call came at three-thirty in the morning. A West Coast radio station had run a tape of an interview that had been aired live a few weeks earlier, and a restaurateur driving home from work at one-thirty Pacific time heard the show and got so excited that he pulled over to a pay phone and called to order the book.

In those days, our 800 number rang at home.

"Hello, this is Scott," was my best attempt at cheerfulness.

"Is this the number to order *Positively Outrageous Service?*"

"Oh, you want to order a book. Please hold while I connect you with the order department."

With that, our "order department" jumped out of bed, added slippers to her birthday suit, and sprinted for the kitchen and an order pad.

Within minutes, my sweetie had taken the order and promised immediate shipping. She was about to hang up when the caller asked, "Was the guy who answered the phone the author?"

"Yes, he is. I bet you didn't expect him to be working in the phone center at this hour, did you?" (Melanie is such a kidder!)

"No. But do you think I could talk to him for a minute?"

"Sure. I'll get him up—I mean, I'll put him on!"

And there I stood, at 3:40 A.M., shifting from one cold foot to the other, giving advice on how to love on your customer.

Mail

If you intend to do business by mail, check first to see if the company has a street address. While this does not guarantee respectability, a company doing business from a post office box should be immediately suspect.

Parcel Post, Common Carrier

The mail order business thrives today. Long-established, highly reputable companies like L. L. Bean and Land's End offer high-quality merchandise at reasonable prices, with integrity and service.

Shipping and handling are key when dealing with mail order, parcel post, and common carrier freight. A dog-eared page of a catalogue on my desk shows a beautiful, not-too-expensive desk that I've been salivating over for several months. The sticking point: the freight charge, which requires a degree in voodoo economics to calculate.

A similar desk is available at a dealer in a nearby town. They offer free delivery, although the price tag is just a bit higher. At the first sign of a sale, this catalogue may lose its place on my desk.

Home Care

If you're willing to pay, you can get almost any service performed right in your home. Gardening and housekeeping are traditional, but today you can get a windshield replaced on your automobile or even medical services, such as dialysis and x-rays, that not long ago would have been impossible. In many cases these newly available home services do not cost more than having them done in a traditional setting.

The key to in-home service: personal referral. A legion of well-trained, well-mannered, all-around-nice people can be found to work in your home. A similarly sized group of slackards and rip-off artists inhabit this turf, too. The general rule: If you wouldn't be comfortable inviting them to dinner or introducing them to Mom, don't let them into your home.

Home Delivery

If you want better service from home delivery people:

- Post your street or apartment number where it can be seen clearly.
- Leave the light on after dark.
- Tip for good service.

Melissa!

We had one customer our drivers competed to serve. Her name was Melissa. Just mentioning it made the drivers jump.

The first time we delivered to Melissa, she came to the door in a sheer nightie, apologizing that she was just getting dressed and didn't expect us to be so fast.

The second delivery somehow managed to catch Melissa just coming out of the shower. Again, we were just too fast.

It's a funny thing how some things can become a legend in such a short time.

By the time Melissa called for her third delivery, there were arguments over who would get to go. When the call finally came, our order taker completed the form and asked, "What is the name on that order, ma'am?"

"Melissa."

"Melissa!"

A pause.

"We'll be right out!"

Cooler heads prevailed. Melissa on this visit was once again surprised. This time she had been sunbathing — nude.

Only this time, the driver we sent was my mom.

Melissa never called again.

Walk-in Service

In this traditional retail shopping and service, look for hours, convenient location, and the number of people available to wait on you. As consumers demand lower and lower prices, retailers squeeze costs by fielding fewer clerks per square foot. In my view, price shopping is killing service in America.

Avoid any place that has stations for a dozen clerks but opens only two or three.

A friend in the theater business tells this story about a woman who walked up to one end of a multiposition concession stand. The clerk, who was the only clerk on duty, had ensconced herself firmly at the center position.

"You'll have to come down here, ma'am," was the clerk's greeting.

"You'll have to come down here if you want my money," was what seems to be the perfect reply.

Any place that has a waiting time of more than a few minutes doesn't deserve your business. This includes auto repair, medical services, and most restaurants.

Also think about this: If every day a business completes the amount of work that comes in the door, why should it take several days for it to be your turn? Why should you be asked to bring your car in at 7 A.M. and then be told that a two-hour repair job won't be completed until three days later? If it's a two-hour job and they know they can't get to it for three days, why not enjoy the convenience of your own transportation for another couple of days?

Smart shoppers do not patronize businesses that are disrespectful of their time.

Concerned business people understand this and make it a matter of principle to complete within twenty-four hours every job they accept. Special-order parts or tests should be the only reason for an exception.

Labor is one of the first places businesses cut to save

dollars. As retailers put ever fewer clerks on the sales floor, instead of personal assistance you get something called a "service island." A service island is another way of saying "You're on your own, baby."

Labor is expensive. If you want service, be prepared to pay. Boutiques, known for both eclectic selection and personal, sometimes elegant service, will by nature be more expensive than a discount department store.

If you are after toilet paper, shop anywhere it is sold cheap. If you are after a special outfit, be prepared to pay a little more for something truly special.

Speaking of respect for your time, Mike Bennett of Classic Air Conditioning in Sarasota, Florida, offers an unusual guarantee: "We promise to be at your home or office within 15 minutes of our appointment time or you won't be billed for the service charge." A neat way of saying that Classic Air Conditioning will respect your time.

After reading *Positively Outrageous Service,* Mike says that if his service personnel are certain they will be more than fifteen minutes late, they are empowered to stop and purchase a bud vase as an apology.

I don't know what Mike charges for his company's service, but who wouldn't be willing to pay a little extra to work with a company like that!

Drive-through

The ultimate in spur-of-the-moment convenience is the drive-through. Unfortunately, that never-leave-your-automotive-cocoon convenience often offers an aggravating increase in order-filling errors and at least the perception of worse-than-usual service.

Drive-through service seems cold and impersonal because it is. You talk to a metal box; they talk to a disembodied voice filtered through a mix of racing diesel engines, ventilation equipment, and who knows what. The best defense: Park and go inside. The second-best defense: Turn off your engine, speak clearly, and be as pleasant as possible. And don't forget to roll down your window — you wouldn't believe the number of folks who try to talk through a closed window, or drive through in the wrong direction and then curse the clerk for mispositioning the building.

I swear, we've had kidnappers drive through and allow their victims to attempt to order from the trunk. An ideal drive-through server might be someone who is psychic and handy with firearms.

In Texas we have problems with ranchers who drive through towing twenty-foot horse trailers that they haven't thought about in four hundred miles. Inevitably they roll up over the curb and demolish the outside menu. After the fourth repair to our unit, we finally added an indestructible concrete barrier. Had it been legal, I would have installed a detonator.

I was in a hurry last week and made an exception to my personal rule of avoiding drive-throughs. I headed for Wendy's, home of the best chicken sandwich this side of Arby's.

"Welcome to Wendy's. May I have your order, please?"

"Yes, ma'am. I want one of those wonderful, juicy, hot, fresh, and delicious chicken club sandwiches. And since I am extra thirsty, do you suppose if I asked real nice I could talk you out of a large cup of water?"

She repeated my order almost exactly as I had given it, offered french fries, and announced the total. At the window, a smiling face leaned out the window and said, "I just have to tell you, you've made our day. My sandwich maker and I enjoyed serving someone who sounds so nice!"

In a high-pressure world, the best favor you can do for yourself is to avoid drive-through service whenever possible. Get out.

Stretch your legs. Go inside. Enjoy the opportunity to talk to a real person.

Getting what you want from almost anybody is based on the idea that clerks don't see customers as people; why be friendly or show concern to a voice that arrives over a headset as you bend over to package the 168th order of french fries of the afternoon? Your job as a customer is to be seen as something — someone — more than another order of fries.

Fast isn't the same as friendly.

Fast may be a way of saying "I save you time and therefore I value you." But fast, convenient service is only one factor in good service. It is that friendly "I have a name and so do you" touch that makes the difference.

17 | "No" Is a Dirty Word

PEOPLE who take "no" for an answer and dumbly walk away deserve what they get.

Despite a company's policies and procedures, if you want something, are willing to wait for it, and are willing to pay for it, the answer you hear should be a loud, clear "yes!"

Notice the conditions: willing to wait and willing to pay.

It is neither fair nor reasonable to expect any business to say no to other customers or to make them wait simply because you've made a special request. Businesses must be concerned about long-term relations with all customers. One customer with a special request shouldn't expect the world to stop "just because."

The second condition was "willing to pay." No one should expect truly extraordinary service for no extra charge.

With those two points clearly in mind, you should expect a "yes" to almost any request.

As this is being written, we are expecting a phone call from a nearby furniture store. Yesterday we attempted to purchase an entertainment center and matching hutch.

"There will be a six- to twelve-week wait on the hutch," was the clerk's response.

"I see two here on the showroom floor."

"They're sold."

I smiled. "They're here and I'm here."

"Sorry."

Had there been another source, I would have taken my business elsewhere.

Today I called to talk with the manager.

"Hi! I have a small problem, and I know you can help."

"I'll try."

"Yesterday we attempted to spend money in your store but were unable. If you're standing in that center office area, look straight ahead. Do you see the hutch?"

"Yes."

"Now look to the right, by the two matching couches. Do you see an entertainment center?"

"Uh-huh."

"Great. The good news: We want to buy them. The bad news: I understand that both hutches in the store are sold."

"Well, not sold — on layaway."

"Now we're getting somewhere. I knew you could help. When do you expect to receive another hutch?"

"Possibly as early as Tuesday."

"So I could come in today, pick up the entertainment center and one of the hutches, and pay you cash, and you would have a replacement hutch in plenty of time for your layaway customers."

"I guess that would work."

"Of course it will."

To persistent people, "no," "can't," and "policy" are sorry words.

While on tour for *Positively Outrageous Service,* I made an appearance on Minneapolis television station KSTP's *Talk of the Town* show. The executive producer had asked for ideas to make my segment interesting. We dreamed up a plan to send one of the show's coproducers out with a hidden camera to try out my ideas.

The toughest challenge: to purchase one bowl out of a twelve-piece set. Again, the key words for making this acceptable were "willing to wait" and "willing to pay."

Julie, a coproducer, handled the job. She approached a clerk and explained that she had broken one of her bowls and needed to purchase a replacement.

As you would expect: "I'm sorry. We can't do that."

"I'm willing to pay extra."

"Sorry. It's not our policy."

Julie immediately recognized the power relationship at work and said, "I'm sorry. I must be asking you to do something that could get you into trouble. Who could we talk to that can say yes?"

"I'll have to get a supervisor."

Persistence paid off. In minutes, Julie had her bowl. She offered to pay twenty dollars.

"That's too much for one bowl," said the supervisor. "Let's settle at fourteen ninety-five."

Ta–da! "No" doesn't mean "not ever." To the persistent, "no" means "not yet"!

"Bureaucrats" — Another Dirty Word

Everywhere I go, people insist that in the real world my ideas about service work just fine. But in the world of government employees, all bets are off.

No, they aren't!

Government and union employees are indeed a special case. Their jobs are governed by so many rules that for these modern-day slaves work is just no fun at all. Everything they do requires a code, a regulation, and at least a dozen forms. With these powerless folks, "no" is the only control they can exercise.

In these situations, being polite helps. They deal with a lot of folks who aren't always easy to handle. Letting them know that you are at their mercy also helps, as does telling them in a conspiratorial way that you know they aren't anywhere near the stereotypical image of a government employee.

My gran is a fun person. She assumes that everyone is as nice and friendly as she. Sometimes simply approaching with the expectation that you're going to get your way is all that it takes.

Walking home from the supermarket, Granny passed two employees from the local power company. One rode high in a bucket at the end of the long mechanical arm of a cherry picker.

Granny reared back and bellowed a greeting to the stranger in the treetops. She was spoofing, as though he were high on a mountain.

"Halloooo!" she chirped.

"Halloooo!" he called back, enjoying the spoof and the interruption.

Granny walked on a few steps, stopped, and turned to the men.

"You know, I've always wanted to ride in one of those things," she half said, half asked.

"Well, stay right where you are, lady, and I'll take care of that wish."

With that, his mechanical monster swooped in for a perfect pickup. Granny quickly hopped aboard for the ride of a lifetime. I can picture her now, laughing up a storm and telling the operator that he's a "nice young man" for his good deed.

If being nice doesn't work, simply recognize the power relationship and go up the ladder.

A neighbor of mine says that in seven phone calls you can connect with anyone on the planet. Let's say you want to get a message to the secretary of state.

A call to your mayor yields a contact with a major political contributor who is on a first-name basis with a Senate staff member who works for the senator who heads the committee that oversees the State Department budget. Five calls and bingo!

If you are having trouble at the recalcitrant bottom, move to the top, where the squeaky wheel gets the grease and the bureaucrats are much less intimidated by the rules and sometimes enjoy showing off their ability to put the wheels of government in motion.

A general rule to follow:

POLICIES, CONTRACTS, AND PRICE TAGS SHOULD ALL BE CONSIDERED CONDITIONAL AND NEGOTIABLE.

It was definitely a low-budget project, but we were excited to be adding a dining room to our small restaurant.

The day before I had left the site just as the first framed walls were being tilted into place. Imagine my surprise as I crossed the bridge, straining to see roof trusses being nailed into place, only to see instead the walls removed and lying in the parking lot.

The contractor and crew were milling around, coffee cups in hand.

"I thought I was paying you to put walls up, not take them down," I said with forced cheerfulness.

"The building inspector said to stop and that we needed all new permits. That could take a week or more."

"Stay right there. You'll be building again within the hour."

At the city office, I found the inspector also standing around, drinking coffee.

"Good morning!" — more forced cheerfulness. "There must be some kind of problem."

"You can't build over that landscaped area. Code."

"No problem. I'll make the dining room smaller by a foot to set back away from it."

"Well, the bathroom is too small."

"Excuse me. You approved that bathroom last month when you issued the permit. Is the problem your bathroom approval or being too close to the landscape?"

"I guess it's the landscape."

"And we've solved that problem — I'll move the wall back a foot."

"I think you're going to need a steel beam in the foundation and an architect to look over your plans."

"We both know that what you just now tried to pull is bureaucratic entanglement that doesn't serve you, me, or the people of this city. You approved the plans. Now if there are no other problems to solve, we'll get back to work."

"I think you're going to have to have an architect."

"I think we need to visit with your boss or the city manager on this. I'm going over to the site. If I don't hear from your boss by nine o'clock, I'll be back to see the city manager. Please communicate that to your boss."

Five minutes after I arrived at the site, the chief engineer and his inspector showed up, code book in hand.

"Hello! I'm glad you brought the rule book!" I said, reaching my limit of forced cheerfulness.

"Here." The engineer stabbed at the book with a stubby finger. "Says right here that you can't build that wall over the landscaped area."

"I agree. In fact, we're moving it back a full foot." Now I smiled. "So now that the problem is solved, we'll get back to work. Glad to know you guys are on the ball. We appreciate the advice."

- Bureaucrats love to say no.
- Bureaucrats hate to be challenged.
- Never challenge a bureaucrat unless you have the stamina to fight to a win.

Not all bureaucrats work for the government. Anyone who would rather hide behind the rules than solve the problem at hand can quite fairly be called a bureaucrat.

At a seminar we met a man who lives in Japan. He says the service there is consistently very good but absolutely unimaginative — not surprising in a nation where conformity is a valued trait.

At a McDonald's in Tokyo, our friend, a displaced Texan used to drinking iced tea by the bucketful, attempted to order a large iced tea.

"Tea is medium," said the clerk.

"I want a large, please."

"Please, sir. Tea is medium."

"Well, sell me a large Pepsi, but put tea in the cup."

The clerk turned red-faced and nearly blew an emotional gasket when faced with this off-the-menu though not off-the-wall request.

Finally, the manager was called to handle the "problem."

Restaurants, particularly chain restaurants, are where bureaucrats-to-be go for training. But that shouldn't deter you from asking for what you want, so long as you are willing to wait and willing to pay.

I hereby grant to you the authority to order an off-the-menu item. I give you permission to share a dessert, an entrée, even a chair if it makes you happy. If you want it. If you will wait. If you will pay. Ask.

A customer in our drive-through waited patiently for his turn to order.

"Good evening. Welcome to Church's. Order when you are ready."

"I'd like a half gallon of milk."

"I'm sorry. Would you repeat that? I thought you said a half gallon of milk."

"I did."

"Yes, sir."

We serve honey-butter biscuits. We use milk in the recipe. We sell milk. Just ask!

If you ask for something out of the norm, be prepared for an unexpected result.

One evening when I was working as a cook at a Denny's Restaurant, a waitress placed a slice of apple pie in the pass-through and asked that I heat it. No problem, except that smack on top was a scoop of vanilla ice cream.

"Gloria!" I called. "I can't heat this pie — you've already put the ice cream on it."

"I know. That's the way he wants it." She gestured toward a customer sitting at the counter.

"It will melt," I whispered.

"He says it won't," she whispered back.

"Baloney!"

"He says he got it done that way last night and it was delicious."

"No way."

"Excuse me, sir," I said to the customer. "This ice cream will melt and make an awful mess."

"Just do it, son. Obviously you don't know much about microwaves. They pass straight through dairy products."

"Okay."

In less than forty seconds, we had hot apple pie floating in ice cream soup. The customer was furious and walked out.

The next night I asked Randy Bundt, the cook who had been on duty, when hot ice cream had first been invented.

"Oh." He smiled a sly, shyster's smile. "Since customers can only see us from shoulder up, I just slipped his ice cream off onto a plate, heated the pie, and dropped the ice cream back on top!"

THREE

Don't Get Mad — Get It Right!

18 | When Mr. Nice Guy Strikes Out

"**T**HERE was heavy black smoke coming out of the engine room. We're still coughing it up today," said cruise passenger Sam Mitchener, as quoted by the *San Antonio Express News.*

Poor Sam. He had had visions of welcoming in the New Year aboard a Houston-based paddle-wheel cruise ship. How was he to know that the officers and crew would join the drinking? And who could have predicted an engine malfunction that would leave the ship powerless and adrift until the wee hours of the morning?

The crew, holed up out of sight, never bothered to explain the situation to a crowd turned ugly. Fortunately, an alert passenger was able to hail a passing tug.

What do you think Sam Mitchener could accomplish by complaining to this outfit? Probably nothing other than to waste his time and increase his frustration. Other than an expensive lawsuit, Sam should probably just chalk it up to experience. After all, in a few years it will make a great story.

Revenge, however, is often sweet. Sam should make certain that everyone he meets hears his horror story.

My good advice: Try to deal with companies known for listening to their customers — and potential customers.

Hector Leal, the operator of Chick-fil-A of Rolling Oaks Mall in San Antonio, stares at me from one side of a customer-comment card. Now this organization listens to its customers. Pretty nice touch to have the photo of the boss right on the card! If you don't want to write your comments, Hector will be easy to spot.

Burger King has been telling us for years that we can "have it [our] way," a slogan that could easily be translated as "we listen." One of my readers sent a paper bag from Burger King that touted the fact that Burger King uses recycled paper.

Also on the bag was "Tell Us What You Think. Call 1-800-YES-1800 — Your comments count."

I called.

After a single ring: "Thank you for calling Burger King. This is Annie speaking. How can I help you?"

While Annie went to find a supervisor, the recording asked that I "please continue to hold. A communicator will be with you in just a moment."

Communicator . . . hmmm! What an interesting term.

Burger King is proud to be the first in the industry to offer a twenty-four-hour, 365-day customer-response system. No answering machines, no voice mail. Real live people called communicators, who are empowered to solve problems on the spot.

If you do have to wait for a communicator, a recorded voice says, "Welcome to the customer zone, a place where Burger King breaks the rules to redefine customer service . . ."

When I called, my wait was so short, I had to ask how the message concludes. ". . . a place where you receive prompt, accurate, and courteous service." No kidding!

I was pleased to hear that Burger King customers frequently call to do more than bellyache. Sometimes they offer operational suggestions, or ideas for new or improved products, and, of course, they even take time to praise Burger King employees who give especially good service.

Terry Giles, supervisor of the operation, says that the Burger King 800 line is a resource for the entire organization.

Best of all, from the consumer's point of view, feedback reaches the field in less than a week. Pretty good response time for such a large organization. Giles says that twenty-four-hour accessibility and high-quality, knowledgeable, empowered communicators make the difference. That's her opinion. For me, I think that Burger King is just making good on their years' old invitation to "have it your way." And you can't give the customers what they want until you listen. 1-800-YES-1800.

The Sheraton provides its guests with a Report Card, and the Doubletree asks, "Did We Deliver?" Maybe as a small bribe but probably because they really care, a small box with matching graphics contains fresh-baked chocolate chip cookies. Nice touch!

Pen Foods Supermarket in San Antonio distributes a short survey that simply asks, "Help Us Serve You Better." It's addressed directly to the boss and owner, Norm Pentecost.

Cathy and Roy Young of Houston make beautiful gift baskets, used primarily as welcoming gifts by apartment and office building owners. But Cathy says that her baskets have been used to soothe the temper of tenants who didn't get the treatment they deserved.

The point of it all? Those who care listen.

Service-serious companies don't wait for complaints. Robert Burch, CEO of Carroll Reed Catalog, sent a letter to customer Marti Heil-Carney apologizing for a shipping delay so minor, she had not noticed it.

Marti had this to say: "Talk about good business! I had not even *complained* that the two jackets I ordered in August had not yet been delivered to me! I was impressed and thought you'd find it interesting and great customer relations . . . to anticipate displeasure and beat the customer to the punch!!"

Marti understands and appreciates good service. Her business, Fables Whimsical Jewelry in New York City, offers such service. For example, she once received a package from California that contained a five-year-old piece of custom jewelry with a broken clasp. It was repaired free of charge and promptly returned to the customer.

Here's a surprise note from Gary Fiore at the Danbury Mint. Talk about great service!

Dear "Autumn Hillside" Plate Collector,
WE'RE SORRY . . .

You recently ordered the handsome "Autumn Hillside" plate in the Friends of the Forest Plate Collection and were shipped "Winter Whitetail" instead. Your "Autumn Hillside" plate is enclosed.

You will not be billed for "Winter Whitetail"; you may keep it with our compliments.

Gary Fiore
Program Manager

The Other Side of the Coin

Some business people engage in more or less intentional rip-offs because they know customers won't take the time to complain.

The top award in this category has to go to the slick fast talkers who sell time-share resort property. You know the ones. They send you an announcement promising that you have won one of the following prizes: a Winnebago motor coach; a five-piece set of designer luggage; a grandfather clock; a vacation for two in the Caribbean, airfare included; one hundred dollars cash.

Wow! Any of the prizes would be worth a trip to look. Then

you read even better news: The cash, which seems to be the least attractive prize, has already been claimed.

I'll never forget our trip to a desolate dip in the desert called Fort Clark Springs. We drove for an eternity, baited by a list of prizes not much different from the one above.

What a joke!

We waited our turn in a room with other, mostly young, mostly stupid believers in the too-good-to-be-true.

Our "sales counselor" was a tall, tanned talker who, mistaking me for the "decision maker," insisted on placing me in the front seat of his Lincoln Continental.

"Can't you just picture your vacation dream home right here on the twelfth hole?"

Actually, we couldn't. First, there was no twelfth hole. No golf course at all. Second, even if there had been a golf course, he had asked the question too early for us to have seen it, since the air was still thick with dust. In this parched desert landscape, the slightest disturbance stirred a cloud of dust that blinded the sight and apparently choked reason.

We'll skip to our prize, the fabulous vacation for two in beautiful Mexico, airfare included. "Not bad!" we thought. Who wouldn't want a wonderful vacation in Old Mexico?

The resort destination was another time-share property. We would have to agree to participate in a "short" presentation. The real catch was that the prize included airfare for *one.* To claim your prize, you had to book the second airfare through their company at a rate — surprise! — higher than you would pay for two traveling at regular commercial rates.

For years we were too embarrassed to tell this story. In fact, the potential for embarrassment is what holds many duped consumers at bay.

It was a small franchised restaurant in Florida. The owner, a woman in her mid-sixties, was a real quality fanatic. I was the field representative, newly assigned to this franchise operator. Her place was perfect, except for one small item: The restroom had a condom machine. Not exactly a family image, especially in the early 1970s.

The inspection had gone well until I discovered the contraband condom operation. Red-faced, I asked if she would mind having it removed.

"Do I have to?" she quizzed. "I use the profits to take ballroom dance lessons."

"It really needs to come out."

"Both of them?"

"Where is the other?"

"Why, in the ladies' room, of course. It's my best money maker."

"I had no idea!"

"Oh yes! I don't put condoms in that machine, and they're too embarrassed to ask for a refund."

The moral of the story: Don't do anything you wouldn't want to complain about.

First, the facts as reported by the federal government:

- 32 percent of households experience consumer problems. (*Only* 32 percent?)
- 25 percent of purchases result in some type of consumer problem experience.
- 31 percent of households with problems do not complain about their most serious problem.
- 70 percent of those experiencing a problem do not complain at all.
- Less than 5 percent of complaints about big-ticket items or services ever reach the manufacturer.
- High-income households are more likely to complain than low-income households.
- The young are more likely to complain than the elderly.
- Northeastern households (especially New York) report disproportionately high complaint-submission rates.

- The more severe the problem, the lower the level of complainant satisfaction.
- Complainants reported greater brand loyalty than did noncomplainants.
- Satisfied complainants reported greater brand loyalty than did dissatisfied complainants.

The three main reasons consumers don't complain:

- They feel it's not worth the time or effort.
- They don't know where or how to complain.
- They believe complaining won't do any good or think no one will want to hear or do anything about it.

It's amazing to think that 31 percent of households with problems fail to complain about their most serious problem. Even more astonishing is the fact that folks who complain report a greater brand loyalty. Do you get it? Complaining need not result in a messy scene. In fact, service-serious retailers actually want to hear from you when things aren't right. Otherwise, how could you possibly account for greater brand loyalty among complainants?

They had a problem, the retailer listened and set it straight, and as a result complainers became supporters.

Of course, there are the professional complainers who are never satisfied. If you are one of them, please do us all a favor and stay home.

From our own restaurant files, a few favorite tales:

A gentleman asked that we peel all the skin off his chicken before cooking it. Business was slow and we had the time, so we did it. Ten minutes later he called to complain that the chicken was tasteless without the skin and what were we going to do about it.

A woman called to ask in foul language where her chicken delivery was. My brother Stuart was the manager on duty. He politely asked her to hold while he searched for her order.

"I'm sorry, ma'am. We don't have your order here, and it's

not on either of our delivery vans. Also, no one remembers taking your order. I apologize, and if you will tell me exactly what you would like, I'll see that it goes out right away."

"Well!" she harrumphed. "I'm going to have someone's backside over this. I'm a personal friend of Stan Gross."

"Stan?"

"Yes, I'm a personal friend of Stan Gross, and I happen to know that when you screw up like this it's his policy to send the order out for free!"

Stuart smelled a rat. "Ma'am, there's a Scott Gross, a Steven Gross, a Stuart Gross, and a Paul Stacy Gross. But there isn't a Stan Gross that I know of."

"Stuart! That's the one. I'm a personal friend of Stuart Gross!"

"Speaking" was Stu's soft reply.

Click! The line went dead.

Just as much fun was the lady in California who sued the parent company, claiming that live maggots in her chicken had ruined her appetite for both food and sex.

First of all, maggots couldn't survive the cooking process, not to mention the development time required for fly eggs to metamorphose into creepy, crawly maggots.

Second, an investigation revealed that the lady had gained over thirty pounds and managed to get herself several months pregnant since the alleged appetite-killing incident. Also, she had lawsuits in progress against several other restaurant chains, with nearly identical allegations.

19 | They Shoot Complainers, Don't They?

If you must complain:

- Complain immediately.
- Speak slowly, clearly, and courteously.
- State your complaint in general terms first; find out if your target can solve the problem.

Complain Immediately

The longer you wait to complain, the less impact you have. For one thing, your memory of the event begins to dull. Lodge a complaint naming an employee who couldn't possibly have been involved or citing as fact something that could not be and your credibility goes out the window, along with your chance of getting justice.

The biggest problem with a delayed complaint: Retailers draw the logical conclusion that if it wasn't important enough for you to mention at the time, maybe it wasn't so bad—if it happened at all.

Speak Slowly, Clearly, and Courteously

When you do complain, speak clearly, slowly, and courteously. Your goal: to be fully and fairly heard. It won't happen if you zip through the facts, jumble the time sequence, or turn off your target by being rude.

Half-fast

One exasperating day I pulled my then ten-year-old son aside and, in a loss of composure, shouted, "When I ask you to do something, I don't want it done half-assed!"

Who knows exactly what that phrase means, but my dad used the same line on me when he was exasperated. Maybe he didn't know what it meant either.

"I didn't do it half-assed," sobbed my son.

That did it. Not only was the kid not doing his chores properly, he was trying to get away with using foul language!

"What's that supposed to mean, mister?"

"I didn't do it half-assed, Dad! I did it as fast as I could!"

I rest my case.

Speak clearly, slowly, and courteously or you will surely lose at your attempt to complain.

Almost never raise your voice

On occasion, raising your voice works just perfectly. Sometimes, rather than raising an issue, it pays to raise a stink.

Retailers hate public scenes. So do I, especially if it must be done somewhere I might want to visit again. But sometimes, if you just don't feel up to the whole Mr. Nice Guy routine, or if Mr. Nice Guy is striking out, raising a stink can be effective — and a whole lot of fun!

At a neighborhood hardware store, a friend of mine was attracted to a display of power tools. A cordless screwdriver was on special. He had admired it for a long time, and the discount spurred him to buy it.

A month passed before he had reason to unpack his new prize, charge it up, and take it for a spin. Unfortunately, the darn thing just wouldn't take a charge.

Upon returning to the store, he spied the clerk who had sold him the tool. The clerk remembered making the sale. He even remembered several additional items my friend had purchased. But, no, he didn't have the authority to handle a refund, and unfortunately an exchange was impossible. They no longer carried that model. "Too many problems."

At the register, the store manager refused to consider a refund.

"Your receipt doesn't show our name. There's nothing I can do."

His voice rising, my friend exclaimed, "But your salesclerk remembers making the sale. The price tag on the box shows your store name. What more could you want?"

"Sorry, our policy sign clearly states that you must have proof that you purchased here."

With that, the customer next in line gently pushed his merchandise a few inches closer.

"Excuse me," he said firmly, "I think you should have someone restock this merchandise."

As he headed for the door, the store manager called to him, "Sir! What's the problem?"

"If this gentleman is an example of how you treat everyone, I don't think I want to take a chance. I'll go somewhere else, and suggest that my friends do the same."

Of course, if you intend to make a scene, be absolutely certain you're in the right.

Smiling, Keri Sartell, a lead agent for American Airlines in Des Moines, told me this story:

A passenger on another airline insisted on an aisle seat. Shouting red-faced at the gate agent that he was a frequent flier, a man of the community, and much too large for any seat other than an aisle, he badgered the agent into creating a seat. The agent led the huffing customer onto the plane, approached a young woman seated on the aisle, and said, "Excuse me, but I need your aisle seat. Would you be willing to trade for a window seat in first class?"

"Sure!" agreed the young woman as she scrambled to her feet.

"I'll take it," said His Arrogance.

"No, sir. I think you'll be much happier with the aisle. We want our customers to get exactly the seat they want whenever possible!"

Except as a last resort, if you raise your voice first, you lose. You lose because you've gotten upset, and getting upset clouds your judgment and pulls your attention and argument away from the point.

Power, it is said, is the ability to maintain your position. If I can manipulate your reactions, then I, not you, have power. Don't think for a moment that service workers are not keenly aware of this. Hiding behind rules, regulations, and often imaginary limits to their authority, those who seek to "push your buttons" just for the thrill of it get shivers up and down their spine the instant they notice your voice or your blood pressure rising to the ceiling.

"Don't let the bastards wear you down" is a coffee-cup slogan that says it all. Stay cool. Hold your position. Almost never raise your voice.

State Your Complaint
in General Terms First

When you must complain, wait until your anger diminishes. Then plan your assault with justice, not revenge, foremost in mind. (Revenge isn't necessarily a terrible idea, so long as you get justice first.)

Begin your complaint by explaining the situation in general terms only. Don't waste your breath explaining the problem to someone who cannot solve it.

Keep the conversation light, friendly, and general. Listen

carefully for clues that might help you present your case once you finally reach a decision maker.

"We've had a lot of complaints about that model."

"You're the third person this month to complain about that room."

"Sometimes they'll offer a refund and a couple of complimentary passes."

"The office doesn't open until nine o'clock, but the supervisors are due in by eight-thirty."

"The boss rarely handles complaints personally unless it involves a large client."

Use the first round of conversation to present yourself as a polite yet formidable adversary. Most important at this stage, learn as much as possible. Think of it as a chance to scout the opposition.

One thing you want to find out is exactly who has the power to resolve your complaint. In many companies this is the president's secretary, who sees all, knows all, and 99 percent of the time can solve your problem. The job includes heading off people who would take up the boss's time, and the secretary has a lot of discretion in how to handle them.

Call the company, find out the president's secretary's exact name and title, then call.

My best buddy

Speaking of "opposition," one of the most important tips for effective complaining: Assume that your negotiating partner is firmly on your side. In a surprisingly large number of instances, the person to whom you must complain really is on your side.

In more than a few companies, the person responsible for fielding complaints has carte blanche to make things right. They *want* you to be happy. Someone who is aggressive by nature often makes the mistake of attacking — and turning — a person who started out on their side.

The two simplest steps for successful complaining must certainly be: (1) Assume that the person who is helping you is on your side. (2) Ask, "If our roles were reversed, what would you be asking me to do?"

When you ask "what would you want," the roles instantly reverse. That difficult clerk or server immediately starts to empathize and think how they would feel if they were in your shoes.

In our home town, a small company called !Cleaning Ideas has a reputation for putting the customer first.

We purchased a product recommended by a !Cleaning Ideas employee with the intention of putting a tough wax finish on our tile kitchen and dining room floors. Several months later (of course, long after the sales receipt had been lost and forgotten), Julie Goforth, our housekeeper, set to work on the floor. After much work and sweat, the finish was gorgeous — until the first time our German shepherd, Chablis, padded across the floor with wet paws.

Print, print . . . print, print, print: little white dabs that looked like floor designs at an Arthur Murray Dance Studio for Dogs. The prints didn't wipe up — they flaked up.

Melanie was furious and wisely nominated me to visit the folks at !Cleaning Ideas. I asked for the manager, wondering whether this would turn out to be a story of super customer service or an example of when to use the ultimate weapon (never going back again).

Sara, the owner-manager, attempted to get details from me about the floor. It was useless. For certain she must have thought, "I hate dealing with men who don't know wax from Shinola."

"I can give you a complete refund on the supplies," she said. "A receipt isn't necessary. They have our label on them."

I smiled, just a little.

"And I can give you stripper that will remove what hasn't already flaked off."

"Well," and here followed a pause, "that's a good step. It's just that, having paid money to apply the incorrect products — products you people recommended — I'm not too excited about paying more to have them removed."

"Why don't you let me consult our chemist to see exactly what should be done with your floor?"

"Okay," I agreed. "I don't know exactly what to ask you to do." (I knew exactly, to the letter, what I thought was fair, but why not stick with the Mr. Nice Guy philosophy?)

"If you were me," I ventured, "what would you be asking me to do to make this right?"

She knew in a heartbeat. It wasn't what she wanted to do, but the opportunity to switch places made the right thing easier to see. Sara and her equally pleasant sidekick arranged to visit our home for a firsthand look.

Later that day, two super people from K-P Cleaning spent nearly six hours working on our floor. The result was magnificent, and their bill was paid by !Cleaning Ideas.

The people at !Cleaning Ideas, like folks almost everywhere, are nice people. Nice people respond best to nice treatment. After all, when we're off the clock, we are all customers.

20 | How to Complain by Mail

WHY IN the world would you want to complain by mail?

Consumer organizations offer advice on how to complain by mail, and those tips will follow in a line or two. But the best tip of all: Complain in person.

If you can't complain face to face, try the next best thing to being there, the telephone. In some cases the phone works even better than a personal visit. Top executives who may not take the time to schedule an appointment will often spend a few minutes with a polite caller.

The most formidable resistance you encounter when complaining to an executive by telephone: the secretary.

Keep in mind that the secretary's first responsibility is to guard the boss's time; the secretary had absolutely nothing to do with whatever problem you are trying to correct; you're probably not the first caller with a complaint, and the others probably acted like jerks; and since the secretary is a customer, too, you'll probably be received sympathetically if you stay calm.

In fact, as we said earlier, the secretary may be able to

handle your complaint without recourse to a higher-up.

Another reason to avoid complaining by mail is that it is easier to say no to a piece of paper than yes to a reasonable human being. Also, letters, especially letters to large corporations, often fail to reach their target. Complaint letters are picked off by sharp-eyed mail clerks or executive assistants and sent to "complaint professionals," usually inappropriately titled "customer service representatives." Customer service representatives, my foot! "Try to save as many bucks as you possibly can when dealing with those professional complainers and kooks" clerk is often a whole lot closer to an accurate description.

And there *are* professional complainers.

If you still must complain by mail, call first to determine who in the organization can solve your problem; the exact name, title, address, and as much information as possible about that individual. Then . . .

Compose Yourself

Instead of firing off a hot letter, why not save time and postage and just shoot yourself in the foot? The results will be approximately the same.

A letter written in anger will make little or no sense, and it's likely to generate further anger. What's more, it will serve as such a poor introduction that later efforts at contact will most likely be ignored totally.

When you write, follow these guidelines:

- Keep careful notes.

- Send copies of important material.

- Write a professional, to-the-point letter that suggests a reasonable remedy.

Accuracy is the best policy

What little bird whispers to us when a problem is about to develop? How can we almost sense when a transaction just isn't going to work out?

When that birdie begins to whisper, whip out a pen and take notes. I carry a microcassette recorder, perfect for recording fresh-at-the-moment thoughts. Worse than forgetting details is reporting them inaccurately. The instant you confuse an employee's name, report that you received a product model the store has never stocked, or indicate a time that verifiable records show to be false, your story, all of it, goes straight out the window.

When you write your complaint letter, enclose copies (never originals) of any material you think support your point. Do not include anything not absolutely pertinent. If there is a key word that should describe a complaint, that word is "focused." "Give me the facts, ma'am. Just the facts."

Complaint letters should be as short as possible and still communicate clearly.

They should be typed and on letterhead. If you have a home computer with a cheap printer, copy your letter to disk and take it to someone with a letter-quality printer. The more professional your presentation, the greater the odds that you'll get the response you seek.

Full-bodied flavor

An effective complaint letter should be structured as follows:

- What you wanted in the beginning.
- What you actually received.
- Why you think the reader will be interested in responding favorably.
- What you think would be a reasonable response (including a deadline).

When you think you have written the world's greatest complaint letter, let at least two disinterested persons read it. It's best if your proofreader-critics know little or nothing about the problem before reading the letter.

Then listen to what they say.

If they think it is unclear, it is.

If they think it may turn off the reader, it will.

Everything is selling, and selling is everything. Don't bother raising the flag about the customer always being right. A complaint letter sells the reader on the fact that your position is correct, that you deserve the response you have requested, and that to so respond is in their best interest as well.

Be reasonable

If you ask for something unreasonable or completely impossible, you are likely to get no meaningful response at all.

Sometimes justice is served by a simple apology. Other times it may be a small discount, a refund, a free service call, or maybe just a little instruction on how to use a new product.

Your letter should also make an offer — no, make that a promise. You might want to promise to continue to be a regular customer. Promise to tell your friends who have heard about your awful experience how nice the company turned out to be when it came to setting things straight.

Always assume that you and your reader have a common interest in a positive outcome. Don't hesitate to remind the reader that your proposal is in everyone's best interest.

Don't threaten to withhold your business unless your business is truly of consequence.

Never threaten in the first letter. An unsatisfactory or rude letter signals the potential end of civility. Avoid being the first one into the gutter, because once in, you may climb out but you'll always stink!

Dear Mr. Stout,

Last week I brought my garden tractor in for repair. Your service people were very courteous and promised to have it ready in two days, which they did.

When I picked up my tractor, it seemed to work just fine. I had asked for a brake adjustment and that a problem with starting be corrected.

Two days later, the mower once again would not start. I discovered a loose battery cable connector, a problem I quickly solved for 42 cents.

The invoice (please see the enclosed copy) indicates that the brake was adjusted and wiring repaired. The brake works great, and I am happy to pay for that part of the service. However, I can see no evidence of new wiring, other than the connection I installed.

As a regular customer, I know that you pride yourself on good work at fair prices. I am certain that the electrical problem represents nothing more than a small oversight.

Please adjust my bill as you deem to be fair. Sorry I could not visit with you personally, but I will be out of town for the next two weeks and know you will want to look into this while it is still fresh.

I'll call when I return if you have not already responded.

Sincerely,

Dear Mr. Brown,

I visited your fine restaurant last night with my wife and another couple. We were greeted by a pleasant young woman who introduced herself as Marianne and seated us near the front window.

Because I had a phone call to make at 7:30, I checked my watch. We were seated at 7:25. By 7:30, we still had not received either water or a menu. When I returned from making my call, the situation had not changed.

There were many empty tables when we were seated, so the slow service was probably not due to unexpected business.

Our server finally arrived. He did not wear a name tag, so I do not know his name. He was a tall, thin, blond-haired man about twenty, I would guess. Instead of greeting us, he just stood staring until I finally spoke and asked if we could begin with something from the bar.

Our service went even further downhill from there. It was well after 9 P.M. when our entrées arrived. I have to say that they were hot, fresh, and delicious.

Besides the slow service, what really bothered me was that my wife ordered lobster and was not informed until almost 30 minutes after we had finally ordered that you were out of lobster.

I asked to speak to the manager and was told that he had gone to the bank. After 9 o'clock at night?

We are new to the area and tried your restaurant on the recommendation of a friend. But after this experience it is un-likely that we will return unless you can show us that this was a rare exception and not the rule.

Our bill was $68.53, not including a tip, which we did not leave.

Sincerely,

Dear Mr. King,

I had a reservation on flight 1692 for Wednesday, the 19th, at 4:40 P.M. from Denver.

Arriving in the gate area, I sat on a cushion that apparently had been secured with Sheetrock screws that were much too long.

When I shifted position, I moved but the seat of my suit pants did not. The result was a two-inch tear in my suit. Not only was this embarrassing, but I spent half the day backing around walls.

The worst part of the entire experience is the manner in which your people handled — or failed to handle — my damage claim. It was an old suit. I didn't particularly like it. All I asked them to do was pay to have the pants mended.

That was over three months ago.

Now I would like the suit replaced.

Your television ads talk about how you think service is the only serious issue. Well, Mr. King, here's your chance to prove it.

Frequent Flier

Writing a letter of complaint should have as its only purpose setting thing right. Set things right for yourself, score a point or two for future customers, and give a business an opportunity to learn about and correct mistakes.

You should never complain with malicious intent. Stick to the facts and let the reader decide how to correct the larger problem. It may be a simple matter of training or a small policy adjustment.

Flying American Airlines from Des Moines, I asked one of the flight attendants who was in charge of the cabin. Without a second's hesitation, she smiled and said, "You!"

"I know that stuff about the customer always being right, but who really is in charge?"

"You are," she explained. "Our job is to make absolutely certain that your flight is as safe and comfortable as possible. If you aren't happy, we hear about it. If you write a letter to complain, you can bet our supervisor will call us in. I know one flight attendant who was called in because a customer complained that she was wearing a Rolex watch, which he thought was a bit too showy. There's no doubt about it — on this plane, you're in charge!"

"Pretty interesting."

"And AA also has ghost riders, who pose as regular customers but write detailed reports. Keeps you on your toes!"

"So you folks work together as a team because if you screw up you know someone will write a complaint letter?"

She smiled. "The best bosses also know how to write nice letters!"

Dear Michael:

Maybe I just didn't see them, but how come I haven't received any of the coupons that can be used to reward flight attendants for extra-special service?

Wednesday on flight #663 (SAT to BNZ), I had another taste of your usual great service. Lisa was serving the first-class cabin and doing a super job. How about crediting her with a pat on the back? And if I don't qualify for the coupons . . . send her one of yours!

Regards,
T. Scott Gross

21 | Playing to Win

PEOPLE with little power look for every opportunity to exercise what power they have. They rarely are more than borderline rude. But in spite of a plastered-on smile, you know — and they know, and they know that you know that they know — that it's a contest.

In a tense situation, whether it's grating condescension or an all-out confrontation, the winner is not the one who yells the loudest. Yelling is the certain mark of a loser. Winning goes to those who remain absolutely single-minded about getting what they want.

You Sexist Pig!

Francie Schwartz is a businessperson, intelligent, creative, and sophisticated. So why do male clerks treat her more like a little sister to be tolerated than a customer with economic clout and social influence?

My guess is that Francie suffers from a rather common malady. She is a she. No doubt we live in a sexist society. Men may whistle and stare, but it's just possible that women may

132

be even more sexist than men, at least when it comes to dealing with other women.

Men who call our office are usually fairly talkative when my wife-partner-friend answers the phone. This is not so often the case when women call. You can almost read their frosty thoughts: "She must be a secretary."

Whatever the emotion (call it attitude) you encounter, the smart consumer turns on to the challenge rather than turning off to the server.

Francie Schwartz, like many business people, relies on a computer for much of her work. No computer, no work. When Francie lugged her computer into a north Dallas shop for emergency repairs, you can bet she wanted to know exactly what would be done and exactly how long the repair would take.

"Don't you worry about it, honey" was the response from the male technician behind the counter.

Francie did a slow burn, took a deep breath, and asked again what diagnostic routines the techie would follow. Again the response was that the "little lady" shouldn't concern herself with things she probably wouldn't understand.

Francie went for the boss rather than the throat. To her surprise and good fortune, the boss turned out to be a she. Francie got her answer, but never quite got justice.

What do *you* do when you encounter a server who is condescending, rude, angry, or suffering from any of a dozen counterproductive, possibly offensive attitudes?

Join 'em!

That's right, join 'em. Because if your computer is down and some jerk is the only game in town, you are not going to win your point by losing your cool.

Winners could be described as the ones who get their way. Well, there's a secret trick of mental manipulation that makes it look as though you are in perfect agreement with your service adversary and yet in the end gets you exactly what you want: By imitating someone's mood (this is sometimes called pacing) you can create psychological agreement that will allow you to further manipulate their mood until you get what you want.

Sad movies make you cry. Comedians make you laugh. Surly clerks make your blood boil. In all three cases, you are being emotionally manipulated. In the first two cases, you are a willing participant. Why not become a willing participant in the last case — only this time, why not join in as the manipulator rather than the manipulated? You can take emotional control of almost any situation.

Step one is to adopt the attitude or emotional state of your target. If it's anger, act angry. If it's depressed, act out depression. If it's joy — lucky you!

Stay at this emotional level long enough for your target to begin to feel comfortable. They won't know why they are drawn to you, but, for reasons unknown to them, within several seconds they will begin to feel a bond. That snuff-dipping, bubba-bellied, tattooed, nasty clerk will suddenly show just a hint of bonding in those beady eyes.

Before you propose marriage or a weekend you'd be ashamed of, it's time to move to an emotional state a step closer to the one that will get you what you want. Be careful; it's not always necessary to move all the way to euphoria to get the service you want. Sometimes simple emotional agreement is all that it takes. If your server is angry and you join his anger, you'll be considered an ally and probably get the great service you want.

Moving along the continuum of emotions until you strike service gold is not as difficult as it sounds. Think about it and you will see that every day your own emotions travel up and down the emotional scale in direct response to the people, thoughts, and activities you encounter.

To move someone to another emotional state, adopt an emotion that is not too far from the present state and closer to the end emotion you wish to create. The only hazard lies in adopting an emotional state so far from your target's current emotion that the bond of emotional agreement is severed.

For example, you can move someone from grief to joy but not in one step. To do the job, you'll need to first share their grief. Then move to sympathy. Somewhere in there is anger at the situation. Next up the list you'll encounter a little apathy, until finally you begin to break into a happier emotion.

You've got to be pretty determined to spend enough time with a clerk to bring them from grief to joy. More likely you will encounter servers who are at anger or boredom. These folks are not much challenge at all!

Let's go back to Francie and her encounter with the condescending computer jockey. Condescension is an aggressive form of insecurity. Like the guy who brags about his luck with women, condescension is another way of saying "I'm cool" in the hope that you will believe it.

Here's how the situation could have been handled:

"Hi! I called earlier. Thanks for being willing to help me so late on a Friday."

"No problem. Leave it on the counter. I'll call you when we get to it."

"My whole business stops without that computer. What exactly will you do with it?"

"Don't you worry about it, honey. Just leave it on the counter and I'll call you when it's ready."

"You must have to have a great deal of special training to do this kind of work. Dealing with nontechnical people must drive you up a wall."

"Like you wouldn't believe! People come in here and expect me to divine the answer to complicated problems just by looking at the cover."

"I know what you mean. My business is pretty much the same. What will be the toughest part of the job, the surgery or the diagnosis?"

"Usually the problem is easy to fix — a bad chip or maybe even just a loose connection. But to get to that point, I'll have to . . . ."

See what I mean? First match the target's emotional state until you get psychological agreement, then use that agreement to springboard to where you want to be. In the above case, condescension became agreement and agreement came to at least a close approximation of friendliness.

All this doesn't change the fact that our computer techie also happens to be a sexist pig. What it does accomplish is the desired result.

Stupid Customers

How many times have you read the mind of a server and all it said was "stupid customer" in big letters? The normal reaction is "Well, we'll see who is stupid and who has the money." That reaction is the least likely to produce the service you want.

At an auto parts shop that dealt mostly with repair shops and dealerships, a customer with clean hands, wearing a suit, walked up to the counter. The counter person was certain that this turkey would ask for a whatchamacallit for a white Chevrolet. He wouldn't be sure of the year or the engine size, although he would be able to do a fairly good imitation of the noise it made.

"Hi! Have you time for a stupid customer question?"

"What's the problem?" said the clerk, his smile giving away that his thoughts had been pegged exactly. "Is it making any strange noises?" His smile widened as he mentally enjoyed his scenario of stupid customer behavior.

"As a matter of fact, it does. It goes *rhumphflat, rhumphflat* when you first start it. Do you happen to have a *rhumphflat* repair kit?"

Now it was the customer's turn to smile knowingly.

Pardon Me

We walked into a typical fast-food restaurant, one of those plastic places so conveniently located at every freeway exit. We knew better, but what the heck. It was close, and all we wanted was a scoop of Blue Bell ice cream.

Two young girls were busy chatting behind the counter. We waited.

They continued their conversation.

"I apologize for interrupting," and I smiled, "but when you get to a good stopping place in your conversation, could we buy some ice cream?" All the while I was smiling, sympathetic, with never so much as hint of the sarcasm I felt.

Zap! In two sentences, we were in perfect agreement. In two pleasant verbal constructions, we came to a common understanding that "it's sure hard to get service anymore, what with rude and indifferent clerks that seem to be every-where you go."

The rest of the service was perfect — all because we had discovered a common agreement that we hate bad service. It is only coincidental that one side of that agreement was also the offending party!

I was once asked to define service. Without pausing to think, I said, "Giving customers what they want."

Looking at the definition from the customer's viewpoint, good service must be "getting what you want." As simple as this concept is, it never ceases to amaze how, when things don't go perfectly, some folks get so consumed with ideas of revenge or justice that they completely forget why they came to be involved in the first place. As a customer, your only goal should be to get what you want.

FOUR

The Art of the Steal

22 | The Nature of the Deal

I KNOW why you hate shopping for big-ticket items. It's not the hassle of financing or the inconvenience of arranging to be at home for the delivery or installation crew. You hate shopping for big-ticket items because you are afraid of making an expensive mistake.

You don't want to face friends who ask, "What kind of a deal did you get?" and discover, publicly, that not only were you taken to the cleaners but you fell for one or more of the oldest tricks in the book.

If retailers would recognize, understand, and do something to eliminate our fear of being ripped off, no doubt sales would skyrocket.

On the way to the airport, I remarked to my wife how in spite of its age the old Buick still rode like a magic carpet. The engine purred quietly beneath the still-shiny hood, yet it had power in reserve.

But where, oh where, is a piece of wood when you need to knock on it? Not forty minutes down the road, the old steel stallion coughed and thrashed in a slow and agonizing death. DOA was the pronouncement of the first mechanic we could find.

"I wouldn't put another dime into her," he opined. "Not a cent," seconded his grease-stained sidekick.

"What if I nurse it to the airport? Will that cause more damage?"

"If you can get it to the airport, we'll be surprised. Look, that car is dead."

Check It Out

If money is no object, pick up the phone, call the first dealer or retailer who comes to mind, and simply tell them to bring over whatever it is that your heart desires. Promise that you will drop me a note and tell me about life in the poorhouse, for surely that will be your eventual fate.

If there is a step one to getting what you want, it must certainly be to find out what you want. Shopping without complete knowledge wastes your time and money. For small items it may be no big deal. For big-ticket items it's an invitation to be taken to the cleaners.

Let your fingers do the walking

Don't leave the comfort of home until you have thoroughly scoped out your target. Pick up the Yellow Pages and phone at least several dealers or retailers to get an idea of availability and prices.

SAVE THE PLACE YOU WOULD LIKE TO BUY FROM FOR LAST.

This raises the question of where would you *prefer* to shop. There may be a store that is conveniently located. Or you may prefer to buy from a dealer with an outstanding reputation for service.

Whatever your reasons, save the preferred dealer or retailer for last. You want to appear as knowledgeable as possible when you get down to actually negotiating your deal, so start comparison shopping with the least likely dealer. Let them educate you on prices, models, features, benefits, and service. By the time you've worked your way to the preferred dealer, you'll be much better equipped to negotiate.

BE PREPARED TO BE SURPRISED.

Your initial dealer of choice may turn out to be not such a hot choice. Frequently, slick advertising and fancy showrooms create the false impression of quality and honesty. Sometimes it will be the little family-owned operation in the less-than-prime location that offers the best price and service combination.

Comparison-shop to check out prices and to discover sales tactics and service integrity.

In other words, after you've decided where you would *prefer* to buy, be prepared to change your mind.

When brother Paul set out to buy his first new truck, he started with a local dealer, figuring that the local guy would be easier to deal with and much more convenient for postsale service. If money had been no object, he would have bought there. Unfortunately, the deal offered by the local guy resulted in payments that, particularly for a young fellow, newly married and just starting his career, were way beyond reach.

Paul bought elsewhere. He really had no choice. Perhaps he could have negotiated a better deal locally, but he didn't ask me for advice.

(The day he proudly drove home in his new truck was slightly soured by a phone call he received at work from a salesperson for the local dealer, calling to ask when Paul would be in to buy. Upon learning that the deal was already done, the salesperson unloaded with both barrels, to the effect of how dare he not support local merchants. The mood further soured when the owner of the dealership also called, to say that under no circumstances would his dealership perform warranty work.

(In an interesting footnote to this story, Melanie and I are now looking for a new vehicle. The dealer mentioned above sells the make and model that has caught our eye. It is no coincidence that we are shopping at an out-of-town dealership.)

Haste makes waste

Impulse buying is economic suicide. Sometimes deciding not to buy or at least to delay the decision is the best decision of all. If your car dies, you could immediately buy another, but you could also take the bus, rent a car, bicycle, or walk. A few days of inconvenience may save a few thousand dollars lost to bad timing or rushed dealing.

Look at catalogues, call stores, ask friends, and quiz repair people before you set your heart on owning a particular brand or model.

Speaking of brands and models — buyer beware!

LARGE CHAINS OFTEN HAVE STANDARD MODELS RELABELED WITH MODEL NUMBERS UNIQUE TO THEIR CHAIN TO MAKE COM-PARISON-SHOPPING MORE DIFFICULT.

You've heard the claim "Find a lower price on the same make and model elsewhere and we'll double the difference." What they don't tell you is that no one else carries that exact model number, even though many competitors may carry the identical product.

If you need an example, just look at VCRs. Televisions and appliances are also good examples.

Auto manufacturers play the game when they produce several models of cars from the same frame and basic body style. To confuse the issue — and you — they create variations of standard and optional accessories plus a few minor changes in body style and decor.

I Just Want It

Really great salespeople probe to discover their customer's needs and then show them a product that fills those needs. Sharp salespeople also help the customer anticipate future needs and suggest that the customer stretch a bit for the present rather than discover that today's purchase won't fill tomorrow's needs.

For example, selling a two-seat sports car to a lower-income couple wouldn't be fair if they were obviously expecting a child. Good salespeople will ask how you intend to use the product. They will attempt to learn about your lifestyle, knowing full well that consumers frequently ask for what they want rather than what they need.

Sleazy salespeople don't care what you need. They are more interested in capitalizing on your appetite for fashion, fun, or whatever.

Long before you go to shop, you should have considered wants versus needs. You should also have a firm price limit in mind. What are you willing to spend or do in order to own this product?

My son, Rodney, set a world record for short-term employment as a salesperson at a well-known and respected auto dealership in San Antonio.

"Dad, you just won't believe how they treat customers. They don't seem to care at all what people need in a car. They just sell them the most expensive deal they can qualify on. I know some of those people must drive off wondering how they are going to make their payments."

You Want What?

Everything is negotiable. Most consumers don't think about negotiating, or if they do, they don't think to negotiate anything more than sticker price.

Price, of course, should be negotiated. But you can also negotiate packaging, delivery, financing, options, accessories, trade-in, and service. To you, all of this may seem minor, but trust me on this one: To the dealer these seemingly small items are extremely important.

The retailer who gives you a cut-my-own-throat price on a bedroom set is still able to smile, because he nailed you on financing, delivery, and setup charges.

The auto dealer who beats every price in a four-state area won't be crying into his beer if he nailed you for outrageous dealer prep and transportation charges. These guys are shrewd, and ol' "Dealin' Dave" who claims that he "loses money on every sale but makes up for it in volume" is nobody's fool. He may not speak enough Latin to interpret *caveat emptor,* but he sure knows how to squeeze a nickel.

LIST EVERYTHING ABOUT THE SALE THAT COULD POSSIBLY BE NEGOTIATED.

When I say everything, I mean everything. Don't hesitate to add even minor things like timing of the delivery, gift wrapping, a tank of gas, and so on. The longer your list of negotiable items, the more you have to lose. And . . .

IN NEGOTIATION, IT IS IMPORTANT TO LOSE A LITTLE.

When a negotiator concedes a point, it often has a psychological weight far in excess of its monetary value. "We gave him free delivery but we didn't have to deliver on Wednesday, as he wanted." If you don't really care when an item is delivered, you can afford to lose a point you value little while picking up a service that is important.

23 | Room to Deal

BEFORE you can be really effective at the brass tacks of negotiation, you have to be at least familiar with the concept of "room." Room is a salesperson's slang for the amount of profit in a deal. For example, an item that costs the seller a thousand dollars and retails for two thousand has lots of room in the deal — one thousand dollars, to be exact.

The more room in a deal, the harder you should negotiate. If a deal leaves only a few dollars of potential profit, it's in no one's interest to negotiate at all.

Usually there is less room to deal on low-priced "loss-leader" items. For example, a bottom-of-the-line car stereo is probably priced as close to rock bottom as possible. (The idea behind a loss leader is to bring in the less-than-serious shopper in the hope that they will be drawn to the additional features on higher-price, higher-margin items. This could be a step up to a better model or an additional sale of accessories.) This can serve as a guide for items of a similar nature.

Another way to discover how much room is in a deal is to pay careful attention to sale prices. There is no reason why you shouldn't at least ask for a similar discount during nonsale times or on nonsale items. It's up to the seller to accept or reject your offer.

Of course, the best way to learn how much room you have to deal is to ask. Or, if you know a banker, ask them! Bankers deal with retailers' finances every day.

Historically, some items have more room for dealing than others. For example, the profit margin in a restaurant may be only a few percentage points. Haggling over the price of such a small-ticket, low-profit item as a blue plate special is stupid.

On the other hand, houses, automobiles, appliances, furniture, resort visits, and expensive clothes often have huge built-in profit margins. Buyers who don't negotiate deserve to be had.

HELPING THE SELLER AVOID EXPENSE LEAVES MORE ROOM TO DEAL.

For example, approaching a home builder without a realtor of your own might be a way of giving the builder more room to deal. Normally, both the buyer's realtor and the seller's agent collect a 3 percent commission on the deal. When the builder also acts as an agent, there's an additional 3 percent. Unless you recognize this 6 percent of leeway to deal, you can bet it will all go straight into the builder's pocket.

Similarly, you can create more dealing room by offering to pick up and/or install a large purchase yourself. You can offer to wait until a large item can be shipped directly to you from the factory, saving the retailer the expense of warehousing or "flooring" the item. Retailers love it when you order from a catalogue of their supplier wares, because it offers the opportunity to make a full-profit sale simply by placing a phone call.

Naturally, such factory-to-you orders go for full retail, since off-price sales are purely designed to move merchandise that has been sitting on the showroom floor too long. *Wrong!* There's a ton of room in a factory-to-you purchase. Be sharp enough to ask for a hefty discount.

Factory-to-you orders offer so much room for profit and/or savings, why not use them as your primary strategy? Let's say that you fall in love with a bedroom set that your friend purchased in another state. You look high and low to find a nearby dealer who carries the same line, with no luck. Actually, not finding a local dealer may be good luck indeed. Simply approach the dealer and say, "How would you like to make a three-hundred-dollar telephone call?" Who in his right mind would say no?

Then instruct the dealer to call the number of the factory or wholesaler, which you conveniently provide. Also provide item or model numbers, wait politely for the total, add your three hundred dollars, write the check, go home, make margaritas, and wait for the truck to arrive.

Sometimes you'll have to be willing to do your own installation or setup, but it's worth it.

Let's Make Allowances

When we were young and foolish (as opposed to our current state of older and careless) we purchased a new home. We thought we were being oh so clever when we insisted that the builder add wiring for a future hot tub at no extra cost. Big hairy deal!

First of all, the line he ran was so hopelessly underpowered, it would have been hard pressed to run a coffee maker without tripping the breaker. Worse, our idea of power negotiating must have been quite a source of amazement for our builder. He got not just the last laugh but the biggest laugh.

As completion drew closer, our builder called to say that it was time to select the interior finish and fixtures. This included floor tile, carpet, wallpaper, and the like. He said that we should schedule an appointment at his supply store (one he owned) and feel free to select any group "A" items up to the maximum of our finish-out allowance.

We hadn't even known about finish-out allowance, but, boy, were we impressed to hear that we could select from group A, whatever that was.

Okay, so you're ahead of me. Group A turned out to be another term for "cheap," and, based on our meager finish-out allowance total, we were lucky to do much more than carpet the concrete slab.

Just Say When

Once you are armed with price comparisons, a list of negotiables, and a semidecision about when you would prefer to buy, you're ready to do battle one on one. Actually, two on one may be the better strategy, particularly if you are not by nature aggressive or in certain situations with the potential for tension.

When my brother Paul went shopping for his new truck, he had the foresight to ask brother Stuart, a name sometimes synonomous with "antagonism," to go along. As the deal was being finalized, the clerk presented a contract that (surprise!) was significantly higher than expected. The difference was for credit life insurance and extended warranty.

"He doesn't want that," Stu announced.

"It's very important," countered the closer. "If something happens to you or your truck, you'll be covered."

"He doesn't want that," repeated Stu.

"Don't you think we should let him decide that?" said a frustrated closer, finally directing his attention to the big guy.

"I said," and this time the teeth were clenched and the smile was gone, "he doesn't want that."

The clerk made a feeble, futile attempt to take young Paul outside — to the cleaners. When that failed, at last the deal was signed.

Negotiation begins the instant you and the salesperson first lay eyes on each other. The salesperson hopes it will be love at first sight, as evidenced by the toothy grin and all the hospitality accorded a long-lost pal.

Your job is to set a mood just slightly different from this would-be love-in. The most effective negotiators are indeed likable, maybe even lovable. But they must also possess Command Presence.

Command Presence subtly conveys that while you are friendly, you are also in charge. Informed, focused, all-business in charge. If a single word could substitute for "Command Presence," it might be "intention." Every move, every word leads inescapably to the fact that you have already determined the outcome of this transaction and that a lesser or different outcome is beyond the realm of possibility, so strongly do you intend for things to go your way. In fact, you intend so strongly to accomplish your goal that you can't imagine the salesperson would even consider another outcome!

24 | What You See . . .

GOOD HUNTERS wear camouflage. They want to control the environment. Intuitively we all understand the importance of visual impression. A hunter in poor camouflage may make deer run away.

DRESS LIKE SOMEONE WHO IS USED TO WINNING.

Negotiation winners dress just sharp enough to demonstrate that they have both money and taste. They remain just casual enough to show that they are not trying too hard.

Unless your reputation precedes you, attempting to negotiate a good deal while wearing jeans and sneakers may prove to be just a little more difficult than if you made a subtle change by adding loafers and an expensive watch — just sharp enough to exude an air of confidence without looking hungry to deal.

NEVER USE A HAMMER WHEN A GLOVE WILL DO.

Even in a buyer-seller relationship, the seller is far from powerless. The salesperson can offer plenty of service and other incentives to buy. In fact, salespeople make much better friends than enemies. When our car died, we were able to nurse it to our favorite airport car rental agency.

"Do you have a reservation?" was the question that greeted us as we entered the lobby.

"No. In fact, we're sort of surprised to be here. What you could do for us is give us a ride over to your resale lot."

"Sounds like you have a problem."

"Yep — dead car — but we may get lucky and find a suitable used car at your resale lot."

"I'll have someone take you right over."

Outside we were greeted by a smiling young woman in a freshly washed and prepped late-model car.

"I hear you have a problem with your car."

"Nothing a new one won't cure," I joked. "We certainly appreciate the lift. Will you be able to bring us back if we call?"

"I'll just wait on you, if you like. What made you decide to shop here for a car?" There was just a hint of warning in her question.

"Well, our car stopped here, you're here, and we've heard that rental cars can be a great buy. What do you think?"

"I've been working here for several years, mostly in the make-ready department. I can tell you our cars look good, but, to be really truthful, most of them take a pretty good beating. The oil sometimes doesn't get changed on time, and, you know, that's the most important part of maintaining a car. And when something does break, we usually just do the minimum work necessary to get them back into the rental lot."

"Thanks. I think we're ready to go back to the office anytime!"

The point is, charge in like God's gift to power negotiation and some snot-nosed kid will have the last laugh.

We Now Return Control . . .

Effective consumer negotiating is a simple matter of control. Control with whom you deal, control what you negotiate, control where and when the negotiations take place and in what order. Then think about how the negotiations should actually proceed.

Take it to the top

Save yourself the aggravation of negotiating a super deal only to have the sales manager regretfully tell you that the salesperson overstepped their authority. Before you jump into serious negotiation, make certain you are dealing with someone with the authority to deal.

We've already discussed what to negotiate, but how about a word about where to negotiate? Salespeople like to control the environment. They want you to be slightly off balance psychologically; if you feel intimidated, you'll be easier to handle. So the power negotiators want to get you into a small office where they can sit behind an imposing (to you) desk and take control of the conversation.

If you are comfortable in an office environment, fine. At least consider asking them to join you on the same side of the desk. Better yet, ask if you can use the telephone, then continue the negotiation while sitting in their chair (the power position).

One minor but important caution: Accept no gifts — not a prize, not a cup of coffee. If you intend to remain in a position of control, you cannot be thinking about collecting your "special customer bonus prize" or even feeling beholden because the salesperson sent out for coffee and paid for it.

That twenty-dollar set of designer luggage or fifty-cent cup of coffee could easily end up costing you thousands. Just say no . . . thank you.

When to deal

When is one of the most important considerations in putting together a deal or simply making a purchase. There are certain times when the customer has a natural advantage. End-of-model-year and end-of-season sales are excellent times to encounter a motivated seller. But be careful: Too many otherwise bright people assume that a brightly colored price tag that shouts "End-of-season price-slashing spectacular" necessarily implies that prices are at their absolute lowest.

Think about it. When was the last time you shopped for a big-ticket item and saw a price tag that said "Regular old everyday price"?

There are three critical matters of timing when it comes to effective negotiation.

BE WILLING TO WALK AWAY.

The instant you become unwilling or unable to walk away from the table, the advantage slips decidedly in favor of the other party. Conversely, not having to buy is the strongest negotiating position possible. An effective tactic is to demonstrate your willingness to walk away.

"I'm running short on time. Let me get back to you later in the week." With that and a thank you, walk out.

You don't have to physically leave to make your point. Simply being quiet, appearing to let your mind wander, or even abruptly changing the subject may be all it takes to signal that you are not all that hot to do the deal.

Let the salesperson come to you.

BE PREPARED TO SPEND LOTS OF TIME.

I'm a buyer, not a shopper. It's genetic. Unfortunately, to the trained salesperson, it's obvious. The real wheeler-dealer has patience, or at least the appearance of patience.

My son, Rodney, is the world's greatest when it comes to the art of the steal.

He once horse-traded for four hours until he was able to purchase a used (but top-of-the-line) clothes washer for eighty dollars and a telephone that did not work. (Yes, the seller was told about the phone.) With Rodney, it's mostly a matter of wearing you down. If you've got the patience, go for it.

Recently he spotted a truck that he liked parked at a nearby house. He knocked at the door, introduced himself, and made an offer. After several hours of friendly bargaining, he returned to our house, disappointed that he hadn't been able to strike a deal that he could live with.

I would have given up after thirty or so minutes. But not Rodney. After a few minutes stewing in front of the TV, he said, "I've spent too much time not to make this work. I'm going back over there to try again."

He got the truck.

Deadlines are deadly to deals.

Deadlines are deadly to deals — unless you set them. Deadlines imposed by the seller are more often than not artificial, fabricated from whole cloth as pressure to get you to purchase.

Sales trainers say that all purchase decisions are motivated by fear: fear of not having the item when you need it, fear of not being in style, fear of missing a good deal. It's the last one that gets you every time.

"I don't think we have a blue one in stock. But we could get you a white one by Friday."

"Well, my event is on Friday, and our colors are blue and gold. I don't think the white one will do."

"If I took another five percent off in case we can't get a blue one in time, would you be able to make a white one work?"

You bet!

25 | Brass Tacks

NEGOTIATION is nothing more than asking for exactly what you want in a way that ensures that you get it. Keep these key points in mind:

- Ask for exactly what you want.
- Ask for the price you are willing to pay.
- Ask for the terms you want.
- Never reveal your minimum position.
- Never apologize for asking.

Ask for Exactly What You Want

Ninety percent of negotiations never have to include the issue of price. For many items price is a secondary consideration.

Even something as minor as asking a server to put a pitcher of water on your table so that you don't run out is a form of negotiating. Sometimes the biggest, most satisfying win of all is just getting what you want. Getting a burger cooked your way at McDonald's would be a win. Getting an order for building supplies delivered and unloaded exactly when and where you wanted would be a win.

Get it? Getting what you want, exactly the way you want it, when you want it is a win. Paying a premium price for the extra service is reasonable; getting it for no extra charge is a deal!

Ask for the Price You Are Willing to Pay

There is no dishonor in offering less than the marked price. In fact, paying an artificially high price because you didn't have the chutzpah to bargain should be embarrassing.

Window shopping on the Boardwalk at Atlantic City, we spied a beautiful ceramic eagle in a shop window.

"Let's look" was Melanie's way of encouraging me to spend a little on myself.

Inside we discovered a yellowed price tag that pretty much put an end to encouragement. From the looks of the tag, the $495 price had apparently been a major stumbling block for more than a few tourists.

"Shall I wrap it for you?" ventured a sleazeball salesperson, decked out to look like Mr. T's stunt double.

"No thanks. Too rich for my blood."

"What wouldn't be too rich?"

"I don't know. Definitely not four ninety-five."

"Look, our season is almost over. What do you say I make you a special deal — one ninety-five and you take it home?"

Actually, that seemed like just the right price, but I was so startled that he would come down three hundred dollars in the blink of an eye that I was suspicious. So we left. He followed us halfway home to Texas, chipping another ten dollars off the price with each step he took.

It was a beautiful eagle, and to this day I wonder if it would have been a good deal.

The point is, unless you've done your homework, you won't be prepared to make a good offer or accept a good deal.

Ask for the Terms You Want

In today's paper there are ads for new Buicks at 2.9 percent financing. The small print says that you forfeit a thousand-dollar factory rebate.

If you figured that the lost rebate was really an interest payment, what do you suppose the real interest rate would be? Certainly not 2.9 percent — more like 6 or 7 percent.

But if it's low rates you want, why not ask for 2.9 percent interest without forfeiting the rebate? The worst that could happen is that the dealer would refuse. On the other hand, they might accept.

Terms aren't limited to financing. Terms could be delivery, setup, warranty work, just about any condition that may be important to you.

In a new-car purchase you could request:

- Free oil changes for a year.
- No dealer labels on the vehicle.
- Full tank of gas at delivery.
- Immediate delivery, and so on.

Ask and ye shall negotiate.

Never Reveal Your Minimum Position

The instant you reveal your minimum position, the game is over. What's left to negotiate if your partner knows the bottom line?

The sneaky way for them to get a look at your cards is to

ask, "Do you have a range in which you want to look?"

This is a test. Do you think the salesperson will show you anything at the lower end of the range? Give me a break!

The second card-revealing question: "What kind of monthly payment do you have in mind?"

Now the salesperson can spread your payments and increase your price. You get what you think you want — a low or bearable monthly payment. You also get a free ride to the cleaners.

Never Apologize for Asking

First, there is nothing wrong with asking for what you want. Unless you are holding a gun, the salesperson can always say no.

Amateur negotiators get into trouble when they say, "I'm sorry for offering such a low price, but it's the best I can do." With that single statement, you've established that the price you offered is indeed too low. Now the salesperson will go to work attempting to sell you on a payment amount. In the end, your lowball offer becomes one very-high-profit sale.

Down and Dirty

Negotiating a purchase is a simple four-step process.

- Get an offer on the table.
- Ask for concessions.
- Agree on the deal.
- Ask for concessions.

Get an offer on the table

The price tag on big-ticket merchandise is not a statement of law or a universal truth. It is an offer. As with most offers, you can accept, decline, or make a counteroffer.

Ask for concessions

Counter the offer on the price sticker by asking for concessions, which may include a lower price. But, as we've discussed, there are plenty of things to bargain over besides price.

Too many weekend negotiators get all macho, walk up to the salesperson, and strike out with this awkward verbal hammer: "What's your best price?"

Immediately the salesperson knows that price is the only issue. There are two likely responses: The salesperson, offering quality at an already reasonable price, drops out immediately; or you'll be shown a low-priced piece of junk and then taken to the cleaners, pockets stuffed with all sorts of expensive goodies like service contracts, delivery and setup fees, and charges for options real or imagined.

The better approach: "I'm ready to buy if the deal is right."

Notice, we didn't say if the price is right. To do that would be to reveal that we are a one-issue shopper. So instead we ask about the deal, which includes but isn't limited to price.

We've also established ourselves as buyers, not lookers. Salespersons are terribly frustrated by window shoppers and the economically curious who take up time that could have been spent closing a real deal.

"I'm ready to buy if the deal is right."

"What kind of deal are you looking for?"

List most, though not all, of your negotiables. In this list should be all of your got-to-haves, with a few I-couldn't-care-lesses mixed in to be used as expendable bargaining chips. Don't make the mistake of identifying your got-to-haves. That would seriously weaken your position.

The salesperson says, "I don't think I can do that."

"Well, what can you do?"

The response you'll get is the first-level counteroffer. If it's a good offer (and you'll know because you've done your homework), decide to close the deal, but continue to negotiate before verbally giving in. You never know when the other guy will blink, so don't stop until you've hit bottom.

Now it's your turn to counter. Give in on something minor, but try to get something — anything — in return. You may end up buying a new couch and two dead chickens, but if you got those chickens in return for some I-couldn't-care-less concession, then in the end they have value in excess of their actual worth to you.

Make small concessions big

Do you remember how your kid brother could turn tears on and off like water from a faucet? The little squirt would aggravate you until you let him have it with a backhand, and then he would stagger around bawling like a lost calf until you got in trouble. A miracle it was that the same treatment didn't even earn a whimper if Mom and Dad weren't home. Well, that's the kind of acting skill you need to be a good negotiator.

Practice flinching. Go ahead, flinch!

For those of you who were culturally deprived of siblings, just wrinkle your nose and look as if you smell something truly disgusting. And when you do it real quick and suck a little air through your teeth, well, that's real pro flinching if I ever saw it!

You need to flinch whenever you make even the tiniest of concessions, because flinching gives little concessions huge psychological value.

Practice flinching and then branch out to a few other grunts, clicks, and quiet moans you can use to communicate that although you are badly wounded, you will concede on that point. Then give 'em one of your I-couldn't-care-less concessions.

Once you have mastered flinching, you are ready for our next technique.

Righteousness

Even the good guys will occasionally forget their manners and try something borderline ethical on you. When you spot a cheap tactic, hold the thought, savor it, and wait until just the right moment to casually observe that you recognize slime when you are dealing with it.

"Let's not kid ourselves. We both know that you advertise model P53 as a loss leader to get people in the door. Well, I'm in the door and you immediately try to show me P54. That's bait-and-switch any way you look at it. And, any way you look at it, it's illegal, not to mention unethical. So let's stick to the subject and not try any sleazy tactics."

Properly said at just the right moment, a little righteousness goes a long way toward getting you a better deal. The real sleazoids won't be much affected, but when regular Joes are caught or even suspected of being less than respectable, it may earn you a few negotiating points.

But it's policy!

Just because something is printed doesn't make it so. If you print a huge poster that reads, "It is our official policy that the sky is green," the sky will still be blue.

"That's our policy." "That's the way we do it." "That's the way our contract reads." "We have to charge you a fifty-dollar processing fee. We're required." None of the statements means beans unless you let yourself be led like a sheep into accepting it.

Rules are indeed made to be broken. Rules are guidelines, not universal truth.

Negotiate your deal as though contracts and store policies do not exist. In the end, if you agree and they agree, it's a deal. Policy can be ignored; contracts can easily be amended.

It's amazing how easily people can be led when you shrug your shoulders and say, "It's policy," or "Sorry, but those are the rules."

One night, years ago, I found myself in Claremont, Oklahoma, the home of Will Rogers. They have the Will Rogers Hotel, the Will Rogers Museum — I think there's even a Will Rogers Dry Cleaners. They also have a restaurant named, if I'm not mistaken, the Heritage House.

Whatever the name, I'll never forget the surprise of being greeted, in what was then nothing more than a diner in a little country town, by a tuxedoed maître d', with a white towel draped ceremoniously over his forearm. Below, his fly was open, and about three inches of starched white waved at every diner, too embarrassed, or stunned, to point out his faux pas.

"Good evening," he intoned, doing his best to imitate Lurch from the Addams family. "Do you know the rules?" (The *l* in "rules" had all the impact of an *r* spoken in Manhattan.)

"No. This is our first time here." We stifled a giggle and the urge to mention his open fly.

"We make a different soup every day. Fresh, homemade — from scratch, you might say."

"Sounds good."

"Lot of people think so. That's why we have the rule that you can only order one bowl per person. So if someone at your table wants two bowls, someone else can't have any."

We each ordered a bowl of soup. No point in letting someone else get all the good stuff.

In the meantime, Lurch was probably bursting through the kitchen saying, "Just sold another four bowls of that soup to a bunch of city folks. The rules bit and the open fly get 'em every time!"

Whenever someone mentions policy or rules, remember that story and order what you want.

Agree on the deal

Once you agree in principle, the dealing isn't quite finished. No deal is done until the paperwork is signed and cash has changed hands. Even then, it's still possible to grab an extra concession or two.

When both parties agree verbally, it's time to put complex or big-money deals in writing. For some shady operator, here's actually where the dealing begins. (We'll have more on that in the next chapter.)

Ask for concessions

The best time to close on major points is right after you have conceded some minor point. In the mind of negotiators on both sides, the value of a concession is obscured by the fact that it was made. Now, basking in the glow of a minor win, your partner will feel good about closing the deal, which makes it the perfect time to ask for one or two additional small concessions. Their attitude will be, "What the heck, we've got a deal, and those are insignificant items." When good feelings are at their peak is the time to attempt to extract another small concession or two.

Your negotiating partner may not catch the disparity between concessions, so toss out a small bone and walk off with the entire pot.

Warning! Over-negotiating May Be Hazardous!

Some folks think that negotiating is a blood sport. But shaving another ten cents off a hundred-dollar purchase is stupid. No, worse than stupid, because overnegotiating can be counterproductive.

If it's a once-in-a-lifetime purchase, haggle to your heart's content, especially if you don't really care whether or not you make the deal. To some, haggling for the sake of haggling is fun; for others, it's just plain rude. To me, it's a waste of time that could be better spent.

As salespeople are pressured into an ever skinnier sale, the incentive to deal diminishes rapidly. Faced with the possibility of a no-profit deal, salespeople (like any of us) are inclined to dig in and refuse to give in even to demands that under other circumstances would have seemed quite reasonable.

Overnegotiate and you may leave feeling quite full of yourself, but all of that smugness will crash around your ears the first time you have to return for service. That salesperson you beat up so badly will greet you with a smile knowing that now, at last, the shoe is on the other foot.

It's okay to be a tough negotiator, but please, leave room for reasonableness. Only a healthy, profitable supplier will be around to provide after-the-sale service.

Watch Out for the Little Guy

In this country we're seeing an interesting shift in buying habits. Folks are discovering that some products have little or no useful service component. With these products, only price and quality carry serious weight in the buying decision. Across the country warehouse retailers such as Price Club and Sam's Club are springing up to give price-conscious consumers the best deal possible on thousands of commodity items.

This is both good news and bad news.

First, people get so crazy over price that they spend valuable time and fuel to drive out of their way, sometimes to save only a few cents. This behavior is truly penny-wise and pound-foolish.

Worse, neighborhood merchants who cannot match the discounter's price suffer. What consumers fail to realize is that it's the little guy who can give you information and other service. It's the little guy who participates in your community when convenience is important. And it's the little guy who won't be around if at least occasionally consumers don't make price the only factor in the buying decision.

On the other hand, the small retailer who fails to provide competitive pricing, plenty of service, and convenience deserves to close. Let 'em go.

Too many consumers stop first at the small retailer, bending ears for hours at a time to learn about the features and benefits of confusing high-tech products, specialty tools, or appliances so they can go down the street and purchase from the discounter who doesn't provide the trained floor staff necessary for truly informed decisions.

This kind of behavior isn't smart negotiating. It's theft. You steal someone's time and talent. Buyer, beware. The long-term impact of this practice serves no one. Someday you'll need that little guy and they won't be there. Neither will their contribution to the Little League, their membership in the Lion's Club, or their participation on the school board. They will have neither the time nor the money for such frivolity. Their new job as a clerk on the understaffed sales floor of the giant discounter won't allow such things. The good old days will be gone. You'll be squeezing the Charmin in hundred-pound bales, and Mr. Whipple won't be around to cheer your day.

26 | Tip-offs to Rip-offs

Y OU WILL recognize the following common sleaze-ball sales tactics.

Bait-and-Switch

One of the oldest tricks in the book, bait-and-switch draws you into the store with a low-price special. In the store, they are temporarily out of stock, they just sold the last one, or, if there is one, the salesperson does everything possible to get you to look at something else.

Upgrading a customer is not illegal or unethical. In fact, as we've discussed, sometimes selling the customer a better, bigger, or somehow more useful item may be the best thing to do. Bait-and-switch artists have no such lofty ideals in mind. And you'll know bait-and-switch when you see it.

Lowballing

Lowballing can be part of a bait-and-switch scam. You are told a very low price but later discover that you have to buy something extra as part of the package or to make the product work.

Lowballing occurs when auto dealers give you an attractive base price for a vehicle and then charge an arm and a leg for the options with which their stock happens to be equipped.

Good Guy/Bad Guy

Salespeople like to play the good guy/bad guy game with their sales managers. You already know that salespeople can't say no to a deal. They usually must clear it through the sales manager. To give salespeople more bargaining leverage, sales managers often play the bad guy. The salesperson, so warm and likable, really wants to help you make your deal.

You will be asked to "bend" a little "so I can get this past my sales manager." Bull! You should be dealing with the sales manager anyway.

Warm Puppy Close

It's harder to say no after you've tried the product. Pet store owners want you to pick up that soft, warm puppy because they know you won't want to put it down.

The same is true for automobiles.

"Take it for a spin," you are invited.

They know that whatever you test drive will be better than what you have. If your old car ran perfectly or you weren't sick and tired of it, why would you be looking?

Some dealers have mirrors mounted in front of the space where you are to return the car so you can see how you and the car look together.

"That car really looks great on you!" proclaims the salesperson!

Aggressive operators will have the purchase contract all drawn up and ready for your signature when you return. Just sign on the bottom line and drive off into the sunset.

I've Got Kids

Some salespeople really do need your business, and a few will stoop low enough to tell you.

"I really hope you like this car. I've got a wife who's out of work, and a houseful of kids."

Sure.

Take it or Leave it

Selling's a game of personalities. An approach that strikes out with one customer may hit a home run with another.

If a salesperson thinks you can be bullied, you may be presented with a take-it-or-leave-it proposition. This is particularly likely if you have revealed that you can't walk away.

It's Sunday. It's summer. Your refrigerator is on the blink and you just bought a whole side of beef. Take it or leave it.

Teacher/Pupil

An older, experienced salesperson and a young, first-time buyer make the perfect pair for the teacher/pupil tactic. "Welcome to my lair," said the spider to the fly.

In teacher/pupil, the salesperson offers to educate the customer. We all want to be educated, and we hold teachers in a position of respect. Here the salesperson takes on an added air of authority, making it easy to lead the naïve to an expensive close.

Limited-Time Offer

Limited-time offers are designed with one thing in mind: to ease you out of your procrastination and into the sales manager's office. Smart negotiators recognize that they are being pushed and hold back to consider options, including an extension of the offer.

Whenever anyone says you must buy today in order to take advantage of this incredible offer, don't.

Limited Quantity

If in doubt about a limited-quantity offer, call ahead to inquire about stock levels. This ruse resembles bait-and-switch.

Undisclosed Extras

You compared price, quality, service, and convenience and then spent hours negotiating the perfect deal — perfect until you were ready to sign the contract. There at the top of the contract is the agreed-on price, but what are all those figures between the top price and the much larger bottom line?

Less-than-honest retailers frequently let the amateur negotiator pretty much have their way, knowing that in the warm afterglow of a successful negotiation they probably won't kick too hard over "standard charges" that are "always added" — charges for freight, dealer prep, title fees, and, of course, automatic rustproofing. And who would want to forgo the safety of an extended warranty?

WHEN NEGOTIATING, ALWAYS TALK IN TERMS OF OUT-THE-DOOR PRICING.

Buyers who make the mistake of negotiating a payment rather than a price may be confronted with an unitemized contract that reflects the payment schedule but not the individual prices of products and services. An uninformed buyer can easily be bumped to a finance plan that gets the payment down into the affordable range but extends a full year longer than necessary.

NEVER NEGOTIATE A PAYMENT.

Buyers who negotiate a payment are often surprised to find themselves presented with a contract that requires higher-than-bargained payments. The usual response: "Based on your small down payment, this is the best figure our finance guy could get approved. You wouldn't let a lousy dollar per day keep you from owning the car you really want, would you?"

Well, a lousy dollar per day over sixty-month financing adds a whopping $1,825 to your total — not exactly small change.

BEFORE SIGNING, CALCULATE THE IMPACT OF EVEN SMALL CHANGES TO THE PAYMENT OVER THE LIFE OF THE LOAN.

Bogus Extras

It's easy for amateurs to get killed in negotiations. After all, the pros negotiate every day, and they know all the tricks.

Sometimes they let you have your price but stick you for extras that otherwise would be included in the deal. For example, you may see a charge for setup and delivery, which normally are included without fee.

Question the salesperson and you may hear "You negotiated a super-low price, and it's our policy to provide free delivery and setup only for regularly priced items."

Others Are Interested

Perhaps it's not unethical or illegal, but you should always be wary when a salesperson tells you that other clients are interested in the same item. It may be true. It's probably a come-on.

If you are told "Another salesperson has a client who is supposed to come in this afternoon with a deposit," be gracious and say, "Thank you for being honest about that. I wouldn't want to interfere with someone else's transaction!"

The Assumed Close

One effective sales technique is the assumed close. The best salespeople believe in their products and truly cannot imagine why you would not buy. To them, your purchase is not a matter of "if," only a matter of "when."

If you find yourself being asked "Would you rather have this in blue or red?", pay attention. You're being dealt an assumed close.

IF AN ASSUMED CLOSE IS OFF THE MARK, SAY, "I HAVE NOT YET MADE THE DECISION TO BUY."

Add-on Sales

Fast-food restaurants sell add-on, or incremental, items. Order a burger and the clerk asks, "With cheese?" Order a cheeseburger: "Would you like french fries and a Pepsi to round that out?"

Add-on selling is frequently a service to the buyer. Who wants a cheeseburger without a Pepsi, a flashlight without batteries, or a camera without film?

When must customers be cautious? When retailers add expensive extras and customers have no idea what they should cost. Beware, because in many cases:

THE PRICE OF ADD-ON SERVICES AND ACCESSORIES IS HIGHLY NEGOTIABLE!

Sales is an Honorable Profession

For some strange reason, I grew up associating salespeople with sleazy tactics and poor taste in clothes.

Well, I'm a salesperson and darned proud of it. There's no bigger thrill than clinching a deal in which you've solved a customer's need by supplying a quality product at a fair price. And anyone who has ever heard my son work with a customer would be in absolute awe of his ability and great integrity.

It's too bad that I've had to write so many pages on how to protect yourself and have so little to offer about the good guys, but here goes.

Great Salespeople

- Ask questions to discover your needs versus wants.
- Suggest products appropriate to your needs, wants, and ability to pay.
- Do everything possible to make an honest sale but never hesitate to send you to their competition if it's in your interest.
- Demonstrate product features and honestly assess their advantages and benefits to you.
- Follow up on service and build lasting customer relationships.

A Southwest Airlines employee, on being commended for outstanding customer service, said it best when she responded, "We don't fly customers — we fly friends."

27 | And the Winner Is . . .

"CAN YOU spell your last name for me?" asked the whiny salesclerk, in a tone that suggested a need for fat pencils and paper with wide-spaced lines.

"As a matter of fact, I can," was my answer. Then, thinking of those trick horses that count by stamping their feet, I couldn't help adding, "Please don't ask my age. I'd hate to have to stamp my feet that many times."

She didn't get it.

In the end, there will always be salespeople so dense that no one will be able to make them move or think faster.

On the other side of the counter, there will always be customers whose only approach is going for the throat. Most of the time, it's the crummy customer who gets crummy service.

For the rest of the world, we can enjoy the millions of smiling service people who would love to love us, given half the chance.

For example, there's the American Airlines flight attendant who dropped a second Ghirardelli chocolate onto my tray and said with a smile, "Just because you are you!"

Or how about the folks with ACT III Theatres who, upon

learning of confusion over gift certificates, sent every purchaser a letter of apology, free passes, and a crisp dollar bill to spend on concessions? Now that is class.

What about the American Airlines pilot who announced, "Good morning, ladies and gentlemen. Welcome to American Airlines flight number 1574 to Nashville. All aboard!," followed by two long toots on a train whistle.

Service on Southwest Airlines is legendary, from the harmonica-wielding flight attendant who accompanies the preflight announcement to the thousands of fun folks who dress up on Halloween, do the preflights to the theme song of *The Beverly Hillbillies*, or conduct Easter egg hunts at thirty thousand feet. So much fun, and not a dime more!

And there's Holiday Inn's general manager, Jim Waldvogel, who gives every guest his home phone number as a personal guarantee that service will be perfect at his Pleasanton, California, inn.

The real service winners are those who work to set things right. After a small mix-up, I called the executive offices of the Holiday Inn Crowne Plaza on Midway Drive in Dallas. Linda Melching listened attentively, then completely won me over when she said, "I've got my pencil. Tell me how I can help." Then she really helped.

Of course, no service book would be complete without a mention of New York City. I always get wonderful service in the Big Apple. I made the ground transportation ticket agent at LaGuardia smile, and she "created" a seat in a sold-out limo.

On a city bus, I didn't have the correct change. "Ask for change, honey," cooed the motherly driver. Before I could turn around, three elderly ladies had produced the coins — and refused to accept payment! (And you want to talk bad about New York City!)

Best of all was the New York hooker who propositioned me in a brief instant when my wife and I were separated by sidewalk traffic. When she noticed we were a couple, she put her hand on Melanie's arm and said sincerely, "I'm sorry, miss. I didn't see that he was with you! I'm sorry!" New York's Convention and Visitors Bureau, stand proud. Your service workers are the envy of the world!

Enjoy the stories, but most of all remember this: Getting what you want from almost anybody has much more to do with you than with them. Recognize the power relationship, market yourself, ask for exactly what you want, and reward good results.

When I arrived at her apartment one Friday after work, seventeen years ago, Melanie was crying.

"What's the problem?"

"The YMCA wants a hundred-and-fifty-dollar prepayment for Rodney's childcare."

In those days, they would have been just as likely to get $150 million as a mere $150. Like most single moms, Melanie was poorer than dirt.

"Don't worry." I held her. "Rodney's not going to be going to the Y. He's going to school out in the Valley. We're going to pick out wedding rings on Monday."

More tears, followed by lots more tears, followed by sobs.

With that, I kissed her and headed for the door.

"I've got to go. I promised my brothers we'd go camping. Don't forget, see you Monday!"

What a romantic! I didn't even wait for the reply.

Oh, well. After seventeen years of being friends, lovers, partners, and spouses, it's probably going to work just fine. That and the wonderful fact that a special part of the deal is our son, Rodney.

Just proves the point: Getting what you want is also a matter of luck!

28 | Negotiator's Notes

Principles of Consumer Negotiation

Prepare

- Comparison-shop for price, quality, service, convenience.
- Examine personal motives: needs versus wants.
- Set limits to price, payment, inconvenience.
- Decide where you think you want to buy.
- List everything that could be negotiable.
- Look the part.
- Take along help if you are not aggressive.

Control

- Accept no gifts.
- Deal only with decision makers.
- Negotiate on your turf, if possible.
- Be willing to walk away, be quiet, or take a break.
- Honor no deadlines. Let time work for you.

Ask

- Ask for exactly what you want and a little more.
- Be specific about price, quality, service, and terms.
- Be reasonable.
- Never reveal a range or minimum.
- Never apologize for asking.
- Be ready to buy if the price is right.

React

- Ask for concessions.
- Make small concessions big.
- Flinch when appropriate.
- Expose dirty tactics.
- Ignore "policy" and preprinted contracts.

Close

- Never jump at a first offer.
- Agree to close after making a small concession.
- Get the deal in writing.
- Ask for something extra.

The Brass Tacks of Negotiation

- Establish an offer.
- Ask for concessions.
- Offer to close.
- Take another bite.

Red Flags

KNOW WHEN TO WALK AWAY, KNOW WHEN TO RUN.

- The advertised item is not available or is of very low quality. (Bait-and-switch.)

- Your low offer is quickly accepted. (Watch for hidden charges.)
- You must deal with two salespeople, one of whom is difficult. (Good guy/bad guy.)
- The salesperson mentions dire personal need. (Guilt trip.)
- You are advised to take it or leave it. (Leave it.)
- The salesperson offers to "educate you." (Teacher/pupil. Beware!)
- There is a limited-time offer. (Negotiate an extension or walk away.)
- The salesperson sells a payment, not a product. (Ask for and examine an itemized invoice.)
- The payment is larger than promised. (Calculate the long-term impact of any change.)
- The salesperson offers a test drive or free trial. (Warm puppy close.)
- Unexpected extras are included in the contract. (Refuse charges or negotiate add-on products or services.)
- The salesperson asks questions to which anyone would answer yes. (Watch for assumed close.)

Nice Guy Customer Quiz

- Do you pay on time?
- Are you loyal to merchants who are especially helpful?
- Do you know the prices you should expect to pay?
- Are you willing to pay extra for service?
- Do you clearly communicate your expectations?
- Do you complain with integrity?
- Do you make a habit of telling about good service?
- Do you negotiate everything?

- Do you ever over-negotiate?
- Do you trade with less-than-average businesses because they are conveniently located?
- Do you use humor and have fun with clerks?
- Do you ever raise your voice or use foul language to clerks?
- Do you accept "policy" as written in stone?
- Do you negotiate items other than price?
- Do you expect good service?
- Do you ever ask for more than your share of attention?
- Do you ever serve yourself?
- Do you usually choose drive-through instead of going inside?
- Do you frequently call clerks by name and encourage them to call you by name?
- Do you say you need it Wednesday when you really need it by Friday?

About the Cover

We thought it would be fun to use people who have actually honored us with their good service. On the right, flexing her way into the shot, is Jody McCulley, who along with her husband, Bob, owns and operates the Kerrville Fitness Center in beautiful Kerrville, Texas.

Holding flowers that were provided by our friends at the Especially Yours flower shop is Donna Bryant. We call her Sunny, for reasons that will be obvious if she answers when you call our office. She is a wonderful videographer, a tremendous asset to our video production business.

The contractor in the center is known by local students as Coach Kaiser. (You can call him Allen.) He built our house, turning a drawing on a napkin into a work of art.

The paramedic is my brother Stuart. Stuart also manages our restaurant. In both jobs, Stuart is one of the most caring people on the planet.

Next to Stu is Matilde. Her mom calls her Mati (*Shh*, she's playing hooky to be in the picture!). Mati is a student at Center Point High School, where I serve on the school board.

The armed and dangerous hairstylist is David Jackson, who cuts what's left of my hair. He's also known as Snuffy Smith, our world-famous radio DJ. In small towns, we all wear more than one hat!

The photo was taken by one of the most agreeable photographers in the West, James Partain. Supervising was my sweetie, Melanie, and Mom (you can call her Shortcake) was making monkey faces off camera.

About the Author

How to Get What You Want from Almost Anybody is written by the Original Mr. Nice Guy, T. Scott Gross. Scott is known worldwide as the originator of "Positively Outrageous Service" and each year delights people from all walks of life with his dynamic presentations.

Scott Gross is a nationally recognized speaker/consultant to some of America's largest corporations and associations. Best known for his gentle humor and amazing ability to communicate complex ideas simply, he speaks in the United States and abroad over 100 times a year before audiences ranging in size from 100 to 2,000 participants. The top-rated talk shows in most major markets around the country have invited Scott to appear on a repeat basis. Scott Gross lives near San Antonio, Texas.

If you are planning a seminar or convention, you need Scott Gross. For more information, or to schedule Scott for a presentation, please call Melanie at 800-635-7524, Monday through Friday, between 8:00 A.M. and 6:00 P.M. Central Time.

HCI's Business Self-Help Books Motivate and Inspire

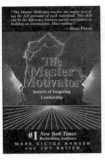
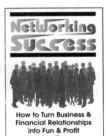